I0840746

Musings and Memories of a Grouchy Old Man

By Robert Dobbin

Copyright 2023 by Robert Dobbin

All Rights Reserved

More copies of this book, as well as my other books, may be purchased at Amazon.com. All royalties earned will be donated to St. Jude Children's Hospital.

Dedication

This book is dedicated to my wonderful wife Sandria, without whom I would not be the man I am today.

Forward

This is an updated edition of my original book written in 2018. I made some corrections, added some items, and moved some to my 2nd book. I also added some remarks based on the 2020 election and the changing political climate.

I recently turned 76 years old and began to think about my life. I never did anything that will be recorded in history, but I think I have had an interesting life. I have had experiences that were unique to me and that I learned from. It occurred to me that my life really boils down to those experiences, my memories of them and the lessons learned and the thoughts I have had based on those experiences. After I am gone, all of that is gone with me. The idea of writing this book is so that when I am gone, others can possibly benefit from what I have learned in life.

Before you read any further, you need to understand exactly what I believe; but please do not stop here because you may disagree with my politics. There are many nuggets here that all can learn from or be amused by.

There are many labels used to describe an individual's economic and political beliefs. A person can be a Democrat, Republican, Libertarian, or Independent. They may be a communist, socialist, fascist, or capitalist. There are numerous ways to look at yourself and others, but I choose to call myself a Constitutionalist. I tend to vote Republican, and I am very conservative in my views, but first and foremost I believe the Constitution of the United States is, and must be, the final authority in this country. I believe it was written by brilliant men who knew much better than you or I what would make a country great.

I am also a very opinionated person. Everyone will find something in this book that they will disagree with. But if it makes you think, I will feel I have accomplished something. Most of what is in this book is just my opinions, but there are some lessons learned from experiences and other pieces I have collected over time. Also, I occasionally researched items online, mostly to look up definitions, dates or statistics. If your opinions are different from mine, that is your right. But if you want to disagree with me on a factual basis, show me the facts and I will admit I am wrong. This is not intended to be a biography, or to be read as a story.

A Grouchy Old Man

When I was in my 20's, if someone was rude or gave me bad service, I just let it go.

Starting about my 40's I began to murmur under my breath about it and maybe say something to my wife.

Finally, somewhere in my 60's I said "I've put up with this s#&* all my life and I won't take it anymore!"

That is when they started calling me a grouchy old man.

Emotional Thinking vs. Logical Thinking.

Several years ago, I began to wonder how people could believe the way they did on political issues. The truth about such matters seemed so clear to me, it did not make sense that others could not see it. Then, one day, I began to understand.

When I was young, I used to hear it said "think with your head, not with your heart." I understood the meaning of this, but I, like most people just accepted it. A famous quote from Winston Churchill said something like "anyone who is under 30 and is not a liberal does not have a heart; and anyone who is over 30 and is not a conservative does not have a brain." From these I first concluded all liberals thought with their hearts, and all conservatives thought with their heads. I soon realized, however, that was not the case. After considering it for some time now, I believe I have come up with the explanation.

Everyone thinks both logically, and emotionally. The difference is how much one side or the other takes control of a person's thought processes. The more emotional a person is, the easier they are swayed to one way of thought or another -

either liberal or conservative. Usually, once an emotional thinker has been persuaded on an issue, their position is set in stone. No amount of logical reasoning will change their mind. Logical thinkers can also be hard to persuade because they have thought out the issue thoroughly before taking a stand. Once they have made up their mind, only a logical argument against it will change their mind. This is true in areas other than politics, even with those who agree on a subject. An emotional thinker and a logical thinker can get into an argument over something they both completely agree on because they approach it from different perspectives.

So, to understand the answer to my original question, you must understand what makes a person either a logical or emotional thinker. I think it is part genetics and part lifestyle.

Is being an emotional or logical person a genetic trait? I think so. A good example of genetics is the stereotypical traits of different races of people. All my life I have seen Jewish people portrayed in movies and television as high strung, emotional people. And from limited personal experience, I find that to be pretty accurate. Jewish people should, by the most logical way of thinking be conservative. Yet they have such an emotional tie to certain issues they are easily influenced into voting for the liberal candidate. Latin people are often considered to be emotional. They are generally Catholic and anti-abortion which most would consider conservative but are easily influenced by their emotions. It is easy for emotional people to become single issue oriented in politics when multiple other issues should sway them in the opposite direction.

Another area that could be considered genetic is gender. Women are generally more emotional than men. In history, it was once accepted that only women could suffer from hysteria or be hysterical. Hence the "Hyster" prefix. Women can be very passionate about their views on a subject. And being generally emotional, they are easily swayed to one point of view or another.

I believe lifestyle influences thinking. The entertainment field is a very good example. Famous actors and singers live a lifestyle that is insulated from reality. They are generally very emotional since that trait makes them good in their work, and it is easy for them to take a particular point of view since they have no idea of the outcome of their views on "normal" people, and they have no reason to care as long as it makes them feel good emotionally. They generally have lots of money, and lots of time on their hands to promote their ideas. The media, along with thousands of people assume, or want to believe they are intelligent just because they are famous. Homosexuals are generally very emotional and tend to gravitate toward certain professions like entertainment. But even people you would normally think of as logical thinkers can be influenced by emotional thinking. A good example is the field of education.

Lifestyle also influences some very rich people outside of the entertainment professions. I have often marveled at business leaders who are liberal. You would think being capitalists would make them conservative. Yet some of them invest large amounts of time and money into candidates that, given the opportunity, would nationalize their business and take away all their money to redistribute to those less fortunate. The only explanation is they are emotional thinkers who are so isolated from reality they cannot see the logical end to their actions.

On the opposite end, being poor can influence emotional thinkers. When you have less than others it is easy to say "it's not fair" and "I deserve" something when you have become emotionally distraught. The logical thinker would think "I need to work hard to get out of this situation" as the only logical solution.

I heard once that you cannot depend on polls because conservatives tend not to participate while liberals almost always do. You can say the same thing about emotional vs. logical thinking in general. Emotional people are more likely to work for a candidate or cause and are very active in trying to convert others to their causes. Most educators are liberal, and they see nothing wrong with influencing students to their way of thought. Homosexuals are very emotionally driven and tend to be very active and organized in promoting what they believe is right. They have been targeting children in schools for some time now to indoctrinate them while they are young. Logical thinkers, on the other hand, tend not to get involved unless they think there is a good logical reason to.

Because emotional people are, well… emotional, they are more likely to take actions or be involved in demonstrations. And those actions or demonstrations are more likely to involve some degree of violence because they have trouble controlling their emotions. That is true for all sides of political issues. Examples are the antifa "thugs" attacking people or property, and anti-abortion "fanatics" bombing clinics, just to mention a few. I would like to say here that there are some groups that are so radical it is not fair to classify them as examples of liberal or conservative thought. Liberals are often quick to say the Nazis were conservatives, but they ignore the fact that the Nazis were socialists. Nazis were extreme however you look at them. Likewise, you cannot paint all liberals with the same brush as the fanatic communist fringe who are trying to hijack liberal thought. (Liberals strangely also try to compare communist countries both past and present to conservatives.)

Emotional thinkers have taken the idea of manipulating speech to Orwellian extremes. The very fact that there is an accepted term "politically correct speech" should scare the hell out of all Americans. Yet our emotions have us accepting this no matter what side of the issues you are on. Ideas and groups of people are given names to suit how they want others to see the issue. Abortion is again a good example. Pro-abortion followers want to be "women's rights" advocates, and anti-abortion followers are "pro-life." Homosexuals want to be called "gay" even though there is no reason to believe they are happier than anyone else.

Speech is tied to emotions in another way. Some people have discovered that calling people names like "racist" is a quick way to cut off debate. (Over the years liberals have succeeded in labeling conservatives as racist in spite of facts to the contrary.) President Obama could not be criticized without someone saying it is racist. Name calling is used by both sides of the political spectrum, but the left has refined it to an art. It has reached the point where many people are afraid to give an honest opinion. If you speak up against the homosexual agenda, you are a "homo-phoebe." If you say you are against abortion, you are against the "legitimate rights of women". Many current comedians make fun of people that they don't agree with politically. People instinctively don't like to be called names and are put on the defensive. So, they shut up. This is no accident. Saul Alinsky wrote in his handbook for radicals that ridicule is man's most potent weapon. This is a real shame as it has stifled honest debate.

Another example of speech manipulation is what I call "feel good" sayings. We have all heard it said "you cannot legislate morality". I remember when I first heard this as a young man. The simplicity of this truth was astounding. Anytime

I could, I worked this into a conversation because anytime anyone said it everyone agreed with its wisdom. However, there is a problem with it. It is completely untrue. All laws legislate morality. That is, by definition, what a law is. Laws are rules established by government, and these rules are enacted because of society's views of what is right or wrong. Or to say it another way, what is moral or immoral. Everyone can get caught up in a feel-good saying, but the more emotional a person is, the more easily they are swayed.

Logical thinkers usually tend not to get involved because they generally see no logical reason to. However, when they are given a reason to get emotional about something they can speak up. The Tea Party is a good example. However, you will notice that even when the emotional thinkers attack them, there is no violence on the part of the logical thinkers, and few other problems. I ask you to compare any Tea Party rally to any of the recent Antifa demonstrations as proof.

Finally, there are people in the world who have learned to manipulate others by playing on their emotions. These are most often politicians, but there are many other examples on both the right and left. I will not give names, but most people know who they are, especially if they are on a side you disagree with. If you have been successfully manipulated, you would probably not recognize it even if it was pointed out.

So, are all liberals emotional thinkers and all conservatives' logical thinkers? No. However, I am going to stick my neck out here and say logical thinkers should all be conservative. However, I will admit some liberal positions can be argued logically.

 Emotional thinkers on the left and right will decry my theory for their own particular reasons. Logical thinkers will ponder my theory and expand on it, revise it, or dismiss it. I guess that is just the way it will always be.

A Democracy

The following has been attributed to the 18th century Scots historian Alexander Tytler, although others suggest, and I tend to believe, that the quote is a composite from several different sources.

"A democracy is always temporary in nature; it simply cannot exist as a permanent form of government. A democracy will continue to exist up until the time that voters discover that they can vote themselves generous gifts from the public treasury. From that moment on, the majority always votes for the candidates who promise the most benefits from the public treasury, with the result that every democracy will finally collapse due to lose fiscal policy, which is always followed by a dictatorship.

The average age of the world's greatest civilizations from the beginning of history has been about 200 years. During those 200 years, these nations always progressed through the following sequence: From bondage to spiritual faith; from spiritual faith to great courage; from courage to liberty; from liberty to abundance; from abundance to complacency; from complacency to apathy; from apathy to dependence; from dependence back into bondage."

It took the United States around 190 years to reach abundance. Since that time, we have been on the downhill side sliding quickly. We are now somewhere between apathy and dependence. Unless we act quickly, we will soon be in bondage.

The Cost of Higher Education

When you want to look at the high cost of higher education, look no farther than your government. Student loans made it very easy for universities to raise their tuitions. If the students, or their parents were paying for it, they would have to come down on what they charge. When your government decided to get involved, the same thing happened that always does when government money is involved; costs go through the ceiling. So, when Biden and others want to give students a "free" education remember, costs will go up and your taxes will pay the enormous inflated cost.

Statues

Black people are offended by statues of the Confederacy, so they must come down! American Indians are offended by statues of Jackson and Columbus, so they must come down! White college students are offended by statues depicting anything to do with the history of that evil America, so they must come down! The KKK is offended by statues of MLK so…….. Oh! Wait a minute!

These idiots need to realize that just because something offends you does not give you the right to destroy it.

Retirement

Since I retired, the high point of my day is going to the mailbox. The low point of my day is opening my mailbox and finding everything is from somebody wanting my money!

Black Lives Matter

There is a big difference between making the statement that "black lives matter" and the organization "Black Lives Matter". The organization is a Marxist group who advocate the violent overthrow of our government to create a socialist black utopia where whites are excluded. (Look it up on their website.) The only black lives they care about are the ones they can use to further their agenda. They have shown no interest in the multiple black lives lost in places like Chicago and Baltimore. They are not concerned with all the black lives taken in abortion. They could care less about the black police officers that have been killed. They also show no interest in the black lives condemned to a life of poverty due to our failed education system or those stuck in government welfare. The statement "black lives matter" has problems too. Are those making the statement saying ONLY black lives matter or that they matter more than other lives? If that is what they are saying, then they are racist. If they are only saying this because a black life is lost due to a police action, then they need to look at the statistics. Twice as many unarmed white people were killed by police than blacks in the past year.

Democrat Voters

It has been pretty well established that many non-citizens vote, and vote Democrat. To protect this vote, Democrats have called for the abolishment of ICE and for open borders. Now, the Democrats want felons to vote, even from prison. To get these people on their side and to vote Democrat, they release them from prison using Covid-19 as an excuse. When they reoffend, they turn them loose again without bail. They call for defunding or abolishing police departments. They order police to stand down, and bring charges on officers for doing their job. But worst of all, they want to take away citizens right to defend themselves with a firearm. If I was a criminal – I would vote Democrat.

Knowledge

Knowledge is a wonderful thing. I wish that everyone had the knowledge to improve their lives and those around them. In the past I have often been too proud of any knowledge I may possess and used it to puff up my own importance. However, I have recently discovered a truth that everyone needs to consider. Knowledge without wisdom is worthless. So, I would say to those out there that are like I was, learn to keep your mouth shut until you can temper your knowledge with wisdom. Your knowledge does no good for others if you just use it to show off how intelligent you are. You just make people mad.

Women's Names

I guess I am just old fashioned. I like the old way of a woman taking her husband's last name when they marry. I get being proud of your family name before you married, but do not tack it on to your husband's family name. Be proud of your new family! Also, we used to have mister, missus, and miss. Now we have just mister and mizz. Mizz underlines in red on my computer but there is just no good way to spell it. Now we have women like Ms. Hillary Rodham Clinton. I get the impression that she just either does not know who she is, or does not like who she is.

<u>Bob Nolan</u>

My first job was sacking groceries in a grocery store. The butcher in that store was a man by the name of Bob Nolan. Bob was a sort of grouchy old man. He kept to himself, never smiled, and talked very little. He had a reputation as a hard drinker. Then one day I came to work and Bob was not there. We were told Bob had a heart attack and was in very bad condition.

Bob survived his ordeal and was back to work in a month or so. But you would not believe he was the same man. Bob looked healthier than I had ever seen him. He had the biggest smile I had ever seen, and you never saw him without it. He was now very talkative. If he had a religious experience, he never talked about it, but something had definitely changed. But the thing I noticed most was that anytime someone asked him how he was doing, he had 2 stock answers – REAL GOOD!!! and GREAT!!! We became good friends after that, and I asked him once about his way of answering how he felt. He said that life is too short and precious to go around in the dumps.

I have never forgotten Bob, or what he said that day. Over time I took up his advice, and now whenever anyone asks how I am, I say GREAT!!! I find that even when I feel low, answering this way makes me feel a little better.

Government Power

We have many in politics (mostly Democrats) that want the American people to believe that if you just give them more power, they can solve all your problems. Recall what President Reagan said. "In this present crisis, government is not the solution to our problem; government is the problem."

Government Health Insurance

In my opinion this country has been ruined by three groups. Lawyers, Politicians, and Insurance Companies. So why would I want a bunch of politicians, the majority of which are also lawyers, taking over medical insurance in this country? Think about it.

Television

When TV was in its infancy, we had 3 stations – ABC, NBC, and CBS. The biggest problem we had most nights was that each station had something good on and it was hard to decide what to watch. Now I have over 500 stations, but nothing worth watching most of the time. Even the good shows run over and over so much you get tired of them. In the old days you had a new show every week with reruns every summer. Now you get occasional new shows and perpetual reruns. A good thing is we now can own movies on DVDs to watch rather than TV, but it is getting to where fewer and fewer of those are worth watching.

Depending on the Government

During the Great Depression, FDR did very little to help businesses recover. His solution was to put as many people as possible to work for the government. Since that time Democrats have worked very hard to make as many people reliant on the government as possible. Alexander Hamilton said in Federalist 79, "a power over a man's subsistence amounts to a power over his will." If you depend on the government for your living, you vote Democrat to keep that living.

Music

When I was young, I did some pretty stupid things just like most teens. But now that I am old, I have earned the right to criticize youth just the same as I was criticized. To the youth of today I say – TURN DOWN THAT MUSIC!!! I understand enjoying music. I did, and still do. But to have it so loud it vibrates windows for a half a block or more is ridiculous. Speaking of music, RAP is not music. It is just some jerk who could not make a living otherwise getting rich by chanting profanities along with a beat. And the recording studios that are making money off of these foul-mouthed jerks should be put out of business. And shouldn't it be illegal for anyone to play it so loud in their cars that the young children in the car next to them at a traffic light can hear this profanity? Whatever happened to common courtesy?

Eggs

When I was young eggs came in three sizes – small, medium and large. Somewhere along the line that was changed to medium, large, and extra-large. Now they are sized large, extra-large, and jumbo. The problem with that is they are still really just small, medium and large.

Am I a Racist?

I have noticed there has been a large increase in the use of name calling between the different sides of political issues lately. One of the things that bothers me the most is that a person cannot criticize someone like Obama without being called a racist. If you did not like president Obama or his policies, is it only because you are a racist? I decided to find out what a racist is, if I am one, and if that would make me prejudiced against someone in politics that I disagree with.

I used the Merriam-Webster online dictionary to define what certain terms mean. I will start with prejudice.

> **prej·u·dice**
> *noun* \ˈpre-jə-dəs\
> preconceived judgment or opinion

I am using this specific definition even though Merriam Webster has several others. All the other definitions have a negative connotation as do all the definitions I can find elsewhere online. They use such terms as irrational or unjustified. However, the root of the word is to pre-judge, and we all do that. For instance, I am prejudiced against certain foods. I have tried beets and have judged I do not like them. You can say that is not the kind of prejudice we are talking about here. That to pre-judge any person or group of people is wrong. OK, I am prejudiced against a group of people called burglars. I have worked hard for what I have, and I am prejudiced against anyone who would steal that from me. I am also prejudiced against anyone or group who would attack my country or try to do harm to it. So, it is only logical that if I believe the policies of any certain politician are harmful to my country, I am justified in being prejudiced against that person - without regard to their race.

But what if I am a racist? Does that not color my judgment and give me an irrational or unjustified prejudice? Let us look at the definition of racism.

> **rac·ism**
> *noun* \ˈrā-ˌsi-zəm *also* -ˌshi-\
> a belief that race is the primary determinant of human traits and capacities and that racial differences produce an inherent superiority of a particular race

By this definition I am certainly not a racist. I no more believe someone being born of a particular race or with dark skin is inherently bad or different, than I believe getting a tan makes someone somehow worse or a different person. However, this definition does not take culture into account.

cul·ture
noun \ˈkəl-chər\
the customary beliefs, social forms, and material traits of a racial, religious, or social group;

Note the use of the word "racial" in the definition. Does believing a group of people are different because the culture of their race is different from yours make someone a racist? To ignore or try to deny there are diffcrences between peoples based on their culture is silly. So, if the majority of a certain race believe a certain way based on their culture, it is perfectly reasonable that some people will be prejudiced against them based on those beliefs, and if these cultural beliefs are harmful to me or my country, I am justified in opposing it. So, by definition, I am then a racist. In spite of what some will say, that is not only not bad, but normal.

Finally, the term bigot is used a lot lately.

> **big·ot**
> *noun* \\'bi-gət\
> a person who is obstinately or intolerantly devoted to his or her own opinions and prejudices;

If you believe I have made sense up to this point, then you must concede there is not necessarily anything wrong with this. I am devoted to my belief (opinions and prejudices) that any one person or group who wishes to do harm to me, my family, or my country should be stopped. And I am very obstinate and intolerant about this.

So, the next time anyone calls me a prejudiced, racist, bigot, I will just smile and agree. But the next time someone says I am a racist just because I disagree with someone like Obama, I will say they are a prejudiced, racist, bigot.

Spell Check

People today are so dependent on computers they cannot function without them. A cashier in the store could not make change if the cash register did not tell them how much. But the thing that bothers me most is spell check. Just because your word processor does not underline something in red, it does not mean it is correct. People need to learn the correct way to use words like then and than, to and too, there and their, to mention a few.

AIDS

AIDS is a bloodborne pathogen. That is a medical term that means it is a disease transmitted between humans through bodily fluids. There are many such diseases, but I want to make this comparison to make a point.

Syphilis is highly contagious. Although completely treatable and curable, without treatment it will ultimately result in death. When a doctor diagnoses this disease, he is required by law to report it to the county health authorities, who then report it to the Center for Disease Control. The patient is required by law to disclose all their recent sexual partners, who are then tested and treated if necessary.

AIDS is highly contagious. Although treatable it is NOT curable. In 100% of the cases, it will ultimately result in death. When a doctor diagnoses this disease, he is PROHIBITED BY LAW from telling anyone.

Take a deep breath and think about what you just read for a minute. As I have talked about previously in several essays, the homosexual community has become a powerful political force. Because they have yelled discrimination so loud, and so often, they get their way on many things. They see AIDS as something that will cause them to be discriminated against.

Unfortunately, many innocent people other than homosexuals have died needlessly because of it. When I say needlessly, I mean it could have all been prevented if AIDS was just handled the way other bloodborne pathogens are. The way the medical professionals know it needs to be handled. Not only would many innocent people have never died, if they would just see the truth, the homosexuals would realize many of their own would not have needlessly died either.

I can get on my soapbox and write a book about this injustice, but I will leave you to consider what I have said here.

Pharmaceutical Companies

I am not one to criticize the pharmaceutical companies. They have provided us with many cures and helpful remedies. HOWEVER! I think they should be banned from advertising on TV. Also, TV advertising is very expensive. The pharmaceutical companies pass this cost on in the price of their product.

Let my doctor decide what is best for me. The pharmaceutical companies are just interested in selling their pill rather than the competitors. I'm sure the doctors are tired of patients telling them what to prescribe because they saw it on TV.

The Homeless

When I was young, we had winos, junkies, and bums. Now we have the homeless. The problem with that is it makes it sound like if they all only had a home, everything would be ok. While that may be true of some, most would still just be winos, junkies and bums.

Multiculturalism

Several leaders in Europe said some time back that multiculturalism had failed. What is multiculturalism? Has it failed, and if so, why?

> **multiculturalism**:
> the doctrine that several different cultures (rather than one national culture) can coexist peacefully and equitably in a single country.

Sounds good, doesn't it? This is one of those "feel good" things I addressed previously. The problem is that this, like most "feel good" issues, is it just does not work. Germany, Great Briton, and many other countries are beginning to realize that experimenting with the culture of a society can have grave consequences. But let us forget other countries for now, and just look at the United States.

First, what is a culture?

> **cul·ture**
> *noun* \ˈkəl-chər\
> the customary beliefs, social forms, and material traits of a racial, religious, or social group; *also*: the characteristic

features of everyday existence (as diversions or a way of life} shared by people in a place or time <popular *culture*> <southern *culture*>

So, by these definitions, we in the US do not have a single culture but are a multicultural society. There is the southern culture, the northern culture, and as a Texan I believe we have a Texas culture. You can divide our country like this in many ways, but, since the end of the civil war, we have all agreed we are also part of a greater American culture. While most everyone agrees to this, I defy any of you to define the American culture. At one time we might say an American culture was one of hard work and determination to succeed. We could possibly say that Americans, no matter their heritage, believed in American exceptionalism, and the American destiny. We have even believed that everyone had the opportunity, and even the right to become better that they are through taking advantage of the opportunities this country offered. We believed these things as part of everyone being American. Now, with today's multiculturalism this has all slowly been taken away from us. As defined, America now has no American culture, but rather an unorganized conglomeration of many cultures trying to figure out how to get along with each other.

The United States has often been referred to as a melting pot. The reference meaning, we took many cultures and melted, or blended them into one. But no more. With multiculturalism, we have become a society of many diverse cultures that are often at odds with each other. If any culture is one that defines itself as being the same as the culture of another country, then that culture will never be part of any American culture. With the ease of travel today, it has become very easy to keep your identification with another culture. Americans of Mexican decent are probably the best example. Because Mexico is literally next door, it is easy for any of them to travel back to Mexico to visit relatives or "the homeland". While they are American citizens, they identify themselves as Mexican-Americans. Teddy Roosevelt once remarked about the Irish and Italian immigrants doing this when he said "there is no such thing as a hyphenated American". What he meant was simple, and it is still true today – if you want to put anything ahead of being an American, then you are not truly an American. Multiculturalism is simply dividing ourselves. The bible says a house divided against itself cannot stand. No matter your religious beliefs, that statement is true.

I was born and raised on the border with Mexico. When I went to school, children were not allowed to speak Spanish. This was not done to be mean to any group of students or deny anyone their heritage. There are two simple facts. It is rude to speak a foreign language in front of people who do not understand, and to succeed in this country you must speak English well, without an accent. Now, because of the idea of multiculturalism, it is taught that you cannot deny their right to their culture and their language. We even waste tax money teaching second and third generation American children in Spanish because their parents never speak English at home so their children never learned it. This is as absurd as a movement some time back to teach black children in Ebonics. If you expect any child to move up in society, then they must speak English, and speak it well.

There is another aspect of multiculturalism that is much more difficult to resolve. That is religious beliefs are ingrained in some cultures. One of the founding principles of this country is the freedom of religion, and I, for one, strongly believe in this. Once you give government the power to decide which religion is good and which is bad you have started down a very slippery slope. For that reason, I believe we must put up with groups like the Moonies and the Scientologists. However, I do think there are some religious beliefs so ingrained in a culture, and that are so foreign to the American way of life, they can never become part of any American culture. I don't know how to address it properly or what the solution is, but I believe there are some beliefs that cannot ever coexist with any definition of an American culture.

So, let me sum it up by saying if you want to live in this country as an American, **<u>welcome</u>!** But if your culture or religious beliefs are such you cannot blend in, then stay where you are. I have no ill feelings against anyone that wants to be what they are in their own country. As long as you don't expect me to change to accommodate you in my country.

Class Action Law Suits

Have you, or any of your loved ones breathed air in the past 20 years? If so, you may be entitled to compensation! I am sick of these lawyers getting rich on class action lawsuits. Most of them are just exaggerated or made-up issues where the defendant companies will settle rather than pay the expense of going to court. If they fight it, the lawyers know most juries will award high judgments with little or no proof of guilt. Then the lawyers get millions and the plaintiffs each get thrown a bone. I was once a part of such a judgement – without my prior knowledge. I received 86 cents (see below) while the lawyers received millions. Who do you think pays these high judgments? You do. The companies just pass the expense along in higher prices.

Dear Robert A. Dobbin

Enclosed is a check for disbursement of the settlement awarded in the class action entitled "Mayamura vs. Chase Manhattan Bank USA, N.A."

Very Truly Yours,

Customer Service

Chase Manhattan Bank, USA, N.A. P.O. Box 15919 Wilmington, DE 19850-5919
Account is owned by Chase Manhattan Bank, USA, N.A. and may be serviced by its affiliates.

MANCK 011205 03737344 08233

CHASE

Chase Manhattan Bank USA, N.A.   MANCK   03757344
200 White Clay Center Drive
Newark, DE 19711

VOID AFTER 180 DAYS

Pay To The Order Of   Date   December 5, 2001

Robert A. Dobbin   Amount $0.86

***No Dollars and 86/100   Dollars

5369920609034890   AUTHORIZED SIGNATURE

THE BACK OF THIS DOCUMENT CONTAINS AN ARTIFICIAL WATERMARK - HOLD AT AN ANGLE TO VIEW

⑈03737344⑈ ⑆031100144⑆900006400 7⑈

Indoctrination

I am tired of my tax dollar going to colleges and universities that think their mission in life is to take our youth and indoctrinate them into their moral and political beliefs. College professors should teach their subject and keep their personal beliefs to themselves. Or get fired! Speaking of which, the whole idea of tenure should be abolished. My tax dollar pays their salary, so if they don't measure up, they should go.

Choices

The Bible says that as a man thinks in his heart, so is he. A man who once ran a school on an Indian reservation in New Mexico is said to have taught his students that their destiny begins with a thought. While both of these are true and good, I would take it further. I say that where a person is in their life is the sum total of all the choices they have made up to that point. While I recognize that there are things that influence, or even control parts of your destiny, like where a person is born and who their parents are, each of us are still responsible for the choices we made that put us where we are in life.

Our Legal System

Our legal system is a mess. I have burglar bars on my windows at home. Why do I have to live behind bars and not the criminals? The system we have now is such that the criminals are not afraid of punishment. I say keep them behind bars with no frills until they serve their time. No parole. And if they offend a second time keep them behind bars for a very long time. You might say that we cannot afford to house that many prisoners. How much does it cost to keep running them through the system over and over? How much does it cost in stolen goods and ruined lives? We might find that if these individuals were actually afraid of the punishment they would receive, we would have fewer prisons. At least the law-abiding people would have more peace of mind.

If I Only Knew

If, back in 1968 I had made a bet that within fifty years it would be common for men to have pierced earrings and women would have tattoos, I could have gotten 1000 to 1 odds, and now be a millionaire.

<u>**Unions**</u>

I want to begin this with a story to illustrate some points. We will continue the discussion after the story.

George was a successful man. He had been a dedicated union member his entire adult life, and therefore made a good salary and benefits. He owned a large, beautiful house with a pool, two nice cars, and his wife did not have to work outside the home. George had it made.

Johnny, a 10 years old boy from down the street knocked on his door one day. Johnny offered to mow his lawn for a reasonable price, and George agreed. Soon Johnny was mowing his lawn every week. George was happy with the quality of Johnny's work, and told him so.

Then one day Johnny showed up with a man. Johnny explained that he had decided to join the lawn mowers union, and his representative was there to have George sign a union contract. George thought this was great! What better way to educate our youth about the benefits of unions. George signed the contract without reading it.

The next day, Johnny showed up with six of his friends. He explained to George that he was just the lawn mower operator. Another boy checked the oil, filled the gas tank and started the mower. Another boy was the mechanic on standby in case the lawn mower broke down. Another boy raked any leaves and emptied the bag of grass clippings. Two more boys were there to clean the pool, and the final boy was there because in the past when push mowers were used there was a job of blade sharpener that had never been done away with.

George said no. There was no way he was going to pay 7 boys to do what one had done. And he never agreed to any pool cleaning. But within half an hour the union rep was at his door with a lawyer and the contract George had signed. It soon became clear to George he was over a barrel, so he relented. After all, the boys did not make that much money, and he could afford it since he made a good union salary.

Over time, George noticed the boys work quality was dropping, and they spent more and more time playing and goofing off. But he didn't say anything.

Then fall came, and winter. His grass turned brown, but the boys kept coming. Then when snow fell, 10 boys showed up. The three extra boys were for snow removal so the lawn mowing crew could cut the grass that was now under the snow.

George had enough! He fired the entire crew. That afternoon all the boys were picketing his house with signs attacking his character. His neighbors began to avoid him and look at him with disdain. He received a court summons for breach of contract, and a threatening letter from the Department of Labor. The local news was at his doorstep asking for a statement about his unfair labor practices, and his own union threatened to throw him out if he did not settle. One night, his cars were spray painted and his wife's favorite rose bush was cut down.

In the end, George settled. He signed a new contract giving the boys double their previous wages. He agreed to provide them each with health insurance and a college fund. He agreed to hire 2 new boys to wash his cars weekly. His wife had to go to work, and he had to take a second mortgage on his house. The next year when the boys demanded another raise and better benefits, George had to take a second job.

George was a successful man. Until he learned about unions the hard way.

This story is obviously not true, but what if we change it just a little? Suppose, in reality, George was a successful man because he had an idea. He patented that idea and took his life savings and a second mortgage on his house to finance it. He started in his garage where he and his wife worked hard up to 16 hours a day, sometimes 7 days a week. After years of sacrifice and hard work they finally succeeded in establishing a successful business. Let's take it from here.

In the story George could have saved himself a lot of grief had he just said no in the beginning. In reality workers have a right by law to unionize. If the workers in the business George established voted to unionize and brought him a contract, there would not be much he could do.

He could negotiate, but the initial contracts unions ask for are usually pretty tame. He could also close his business, but he would lose everything he and his wife worked for.

In the story, George was glad to welcome in the union. In reality that is often true. Many businessmen believe in unions. I have had personal experience with that. But usually those who believe in unions are small businesses that have not had much experience with them.

In the story, George found himself over a barrel because he signed a contract. Suddenly he was forced to employ unwanted and unneeded workers. Without taking the time to go into detail, let me say that every one of the six extra boys in the story come from actual examples. Unions are all about numbers and dues. They talk big about guaranteeing work quality and such, but in reality, all they want is more dues paying members.

In the story, George noticed the quality of work going down and time being spent goofing off. This is the reality of unions. Once the worker realizes his job is protected even if he does poor work or goofs off, it is just human nature to slack off. And in reality, when the workers slack off, the cost of doing business goes up. I'll give you the example of General Motors. (Or as I like to call them, Government Motors.) Do you really think that car you bought from GM is worth $30,000? And don't you get tired of taking it in to the shop over and over?

In the story, when the work slowed down because of the change in the season, George could not lay off some of his work force. In fact, he had to hire extra workers. This is again true in reality. Once again, unions are all about numbers and dues.

Now the fun begins. Let us say that in reality, George has had enough! After all, it was his idea. It was financed with his money. He and his wife worked very hard to establish their business. Doesn't he have the right to run it the way he believes it should be run? According to the unions, no. The unions say he is getting rich off the backs of the honest working man. However, George decided to challenge them, and lays them all off.

The first weapon unions use when they don't get their way is the strike. Striking is a tactic that is basically bullying and blackmail. The goal is to hurt the business financially and turn public opinion against them. The unions also have the law behind them because of the contract the business was forced to sign to stay in business. The unions even have a federal government agency, the Department of Labor, on their side. The news media are on the union's side, mainly because most of them are also union members, and all other unions always support a brother who is on strike. All of this makes a formidable opponent for the business.

If the business continues to resist, the unions take the fight to another level. In the story George had his cars spray painted and a rose bush destroyed. In reality, that would be minor. Unions have proven capable of destroying property, beating individuals, and even on occasion, murder. Unions have shown they will stop at nothing to get their way.

In the story the boys nearly bankrupted George. In reality, it seldom works that way. At least not at first. That is because in the story George did not have a product to sell. When you sell a product, you can cover the expense of union labor by raising prices and lowering quality. So, who pays for the union wages and benefits? You do. I give you GM once more. Does anyone really think the CEO and board of GM take the loss? But as in the case of GM, the unions can finally demand so much that the company cannot raise prices and lower quality enough to cover it. Your tax dollar bailed out a bankrupt GM only because the unions bankrupted them. Our government stepped in because they knew that if it went to a bankruptcy court, the unions would lose.

Finally, the union movement began with the socialist movement in the late 1800's and early 1900's. Socialism can only take hold when they can convince the majority to be unhappy with their current system of government. Likewise, unions can only exist if they keep their members unhappy with management. They must keep demanding more and more.

My father was a very strong union man. He even once passed up a promotion to management because he would have to quit the union. In the end, he admitted the union really did very little for him.

Lies Taught

I know a young girl wh,o when about 13 or 14 years of age announced she is bi-sexual. When we asked her why she thought that, she said she has girlfriends she likes just as much or more than boys. She had been taught in school that that means she is bi-sexual. Our educational system is teaching these kinds of lies to our children. EVERY child of this age has close relations with another child of the same gender. This is normal and not a sign of being bi-sexual. This is just another way the liberals are trying to bring down the moral fabric of our society.

Working for the Man

There was a family in my town who were not just Democrats, but important in the local party. Their son, who was in his late 20's was unemployed and still living at home. To be fair, this was during the Obama years and jobs were scarce. He finally got a job working in the oilfields near Midland, Texas and was making good money. Within several weeks however he was back home living off his parents. He said that it was not right for him to work so hard just to make the oil companies richer; so he quit. This argument is similar to the Democrats not wanting to give tax cuts to large businesses. My question to all of them is this. How many poor people have ever given you a job? For that matter, how many people anywhere have ever made a living working for a poor person? In a capitalist society, people with money often spend a good deal of it employing people to make them more money. If the government takes money away from them, they have less money to hire more employees.

The Only Thing You Have To Fear Is....

I have often said that the only thing a person really has to fear is their own government. Let me explain. You may have something stolen or taken from you, but it can be replaced or you can do without it. You can be attacked and injured, but injuries will heal or if not, you can learn to live with your disability. You can be killed, but your loved ones will continue on without you; and there are much worse things than losing your life. Only a government can take everything you have with no hope of replacing it. Only a government can torture and injure a citizen and deny treatment for injuries. And only a government can take a life with no legal consequences. Your government can take away not only all that you have, but all that you are.

You might say that is true of some third world or communist governments, but in a democracy like ours, the people can keep all that from happening. Do you really believe that? A democracy is only as strong as the people demand. If the people slowly allow a government to take away their freedoms; little by little they will reach a point where there is no way to reverse it. In a democratic republic like we have in the United States, our rights being protected depends on the politicians we send to Washington. But what is a politician? Is a politician someone who really wants to serve the constituents? Maybe. Is a politician someone who believes in our democracy and wants to represent his constituents and their best interest? Maybe. Is a politician someone who knows what is best for our country and will always work to that end? Almost definitely not! What type of person seeks to get elected to government office? In general, you can say it is a person who is very self-confident in their own abilities. He or she is also a person who has a gift of communicating with the ability to make others believe in them. But unfortunately, more often than not, it is a person who has learned to use their confidence and communication skills to their advantage. Politics is all about power, and power is addictive. The more power the politicians are given, the more they want. Once they reach the point where they are completely intoxicated with power, they will try to run your life. So, the only answer is to limit the power of the politicians.

There is nothing more sacred, aside from your religious beliefs, than your right to vote. Let me repeat that. There is nothing – **<u>Nothing</u>** – more sacred outside of your religion than your individual vote. So, voter fraud should be treated as a very serious offence. Most people in this country have no idea how prevalent it is, and the politicians want you to believe it does not exist. Not only does it happen in every election, people sometimes get elected to office fraudulently. There is even one confirmed instance where the President of the United States was elected through voter fraud. No, it was not George W. Bush. It was John Kennedy. More about that later. There should be very strict laws that are vigorously enforced to stop this. I am talking about lengthy prison terms. Any politician found guilty of participating in voter fraud must be banned from ever holding any public office or even being put in a position of influencing public policy. The right of our active military abroad to vote and have it counted MUST be protected. I will say that I believe there are certain instances where a citizen should lose their right to vote. I believe a convicted felon should be denied voting rights, at least for a period of time. Although I do not believe in a literacy or intelligence test, people declared mentally incompetent should not vote. Absentee and early voting should be severely curtailed to eliminate fraud.

When any law is proposed there should be two questions answered before it is put before congress. First, is it really needed? Then, if the answer is yes, what is the lowest level of government that can adequately take care of it? The farther away a seat of government is, the less control the citizens feel they have. Local and state politicians have realized they can pass their duties up so they don't have to answer to their voters. As a result, the federal government has taken over too many things that should be handled at a lower form of government. This also gives the federal government power to basically blackmail states and localities, and yes, the people. If the money for any service comes from the federal government, they can dictate what must be done to get that money and how it must be spent. Or worse, threaten to withhold money to influence another decision or issue. One example is welfare. Welfare should be none of the federal governments business. Your tax dollar goes to Washington just to have them spend part of it for administration then send what is left back to the state with rules on how they can spend it. And the rules are made by politicians who are more interested in having someone dependent on them and therefore grateful enough to vote them back into office. So, no law should be passed by the federal government that can be handled by the state government. And no law should be passed by the state government that can be handled by the county government, and so on down to the city government and school district.

Who is the government? Is it some all-powerful entity residing in Washington or your state capital? No, the government is you, good or bad. The government has no money. It is your money. The government gives no benefits. They are paid for with your money. So anytime a person relies on the government for any part of their living, it is being paid for with the citizen's money. The way it is working now is the citizens that contribute the least, get the most in return. I am not saying any society should not take care of its citizens in need. What I am saying is we should not allow our government to create a class of dependent people who are indebted to the politicians. Anytime a person receives government assistance, there should be a required effort to get that person off that assistance as soon as possible. And wherever possible, the person receiving assistance should be put to work doing whatever is available within the government to repay that assistance. If that means being a janitor in a government office building, so be it. If you live in a democracy, you need to understand it. A democracy is a government where everyone shares in the responsibility. It is not and was never intended to be a system where some thrive at the expense of others.

The politicians have also created another class of citizens. It is the government worker. Any entity of government, and therefore anyone who works for that entity depends on tax money (yours) allocated by the government to exist. Therefore, the government workers have a vested interest in keeping that entity open and growing. No government program ever goes away. It just grows into a monster. A recent study showed that certain functions of government are duplicated over and over and over again in different departments of government. No politician will ever take away any government authority or be responsible for any government employee losing their job unless they are forced to do it.

Everyone that reads this should consider the 2020 election. The 'government" under the Democrats cheated to take total power over this country. If they get away with this, it will be very hard to take your country back.

Henry White

I once worked in a very large facility that included a heavy equipment repair shop. A man named Clyde Williams was the foreman over the shop. Clyde was an older man, close to retirement. He had arthritis so bad, he would hobble down the hall to his office every morning with a pillow under his arm that he sat on. He just sat at his desk all day until time to hobble back down the hall, carrying his pillow, and go home. His assistant, Henry White, actually ran the shop.

Henry was a man of about 45 or 50 and in apparent good health. He could be seen at any time of the day hurrying between areas taking care of business. Everyone liked and respected Henry.

One day while eating lunch, Henry had a chest pain. He went to the shop nurse who immediately had him lie down while she called an ambulance. By the time the ambulance arrived, Henry was dead.

Everyone was shocked and saddened. Henry's death was the subject of most conversations for several days. The day of his funeral, many people took off work to attend. The next day though, something strange happened. Everyone began to go on with their lives and forget about Henry. A replacement was soon found for his job, and the shop continued to operate smoothly. And Clyde continued to sit on his pillow all day.

I have never forgotten Henry because it taught me an invaluable lesson. No matter how good a person is at their job. No matter how hard a person works. No matter how much you are liked. Someday you will be replaced and forgotten.

Day Old Bread

When I worked in a grocery store while I was still in school, the bread trucks would line up before the store opened. They would remove all the bread from the shelves that did not sell the day before and replace them with bread that had been baked overnight. The bread they removed was then taken to day-old bread stores to sell at a discounted price. If it did not sell as day old, it was thrown out and farmers would take it to feed their livestock. Today, bread has so much preservatives in it that it may be a week old when you buy it. I miss the taste of fresh bread from the store that had just been baked.

The Plan
Author Unknown

In the beginning was the plan. And the plan was without merit or substance.

And darkness fell on the faces of the workers. And they spoke among themselves saying "It is a crock of shit, and it stinketh."

And the workers went to their supervisor and said "It is a pail of dung, and none may abide the odor thereof."

And the supervisor went to the manager saying "The workers say it is a container of excrement, and it is so strong that none may abide it."

And the manager went to the Directors and said "The workers feel it is a vessel of fertilizer and none may withstand its strength".

And the Directors spoke among themselves saying "The workers think it contains that which aids in growth and is very strong".

So, one of the Directors, seeing an opportunity, went to a Vice President and said "It promotes growth and is very powerful".

And the Vice President went to the President saying unto him "I have decided to implement this new plan that even the workers agree will actively promote the growth and vigor of the company, with powerful effects".

And the President looked upon the plan and saw it was good. And the plan became policy.

24 Hour News

For many years television news consisted of ½ hour of local news followed by ½ hour of national news. Then CNN introduced the 24-hour news channel. If there was previously only enough news to fill one hour, how do they now stretch it out to 24 hours and keep people watching? Easy. You turn it into entertainment! You drag out shootings, accidents, political fights as far as possible until another one comes along. Have you not noticed that as soon as a new tragedy happens every station forgets the previous one that they claimed was a sign that the end of society as we know it was coming?

<u>**Just Asking**</u>

If all the members of congress that are of European decent formed a congressional white caucus to promote only the issues related to white people would that be racist and bad?

If a Hispanic member or congress, or any other person wants special treatment for illegal immigrants from Mexico but would not feel the same if the issue was illegal immigrants from Canada, would that be racist and wrong?

If you put your race ahead of your nationality is that being a racist or bad? For instance, if I call myself an Irish American.

If you demand that you be treated differently because of your "culture" at the expense of others is that being a racist or bad? For instance, refusing to learn or speak English, and expecting others to accommodate that.

Is having special television networks and publications dedicated solely to one race being racist or wrong? For instance, if I wanted to start a TV network and called it WET (White Entertainment Television) or had another network that broadcasts only in a foreign language. Or, I could publish a magazine called "Ivory" that is designed solely to promote white issues.

Just asking.

<u>Our Military</u>

My admiration for our men and women in the military is second to none. I am sick of seeing them come home maimed or in body bags because some politician thought some war was a good idea. The Constitution says only Congress can declare war. And then, in my opinion, it should have clearly defined reasons and goals. Most importantly, do whatever is needed to win it and bring our troops home!

The Dumbing Down of America

I am not going to mince words here. The public education system in America is a dismal failure. But why? This country has always had the brightest people and the best resources. Why are these not used to educate our children? There are several reasons.

First and foremost are unions. I have written another essay on unions, but for now let us just look at the teacher's unions. Teachers and school administrators work for me. Their wages are paid by my taxes. I don't need some union official protecting incompetent teachers, dictating school policies, or otherwise preventing the tax payers from having what they pay for with regards to educating our children. The whole idea of a union is opposite from what is needed to insure a good education for our children. Teachers should not be allowed to unionize.

The next problem is attitude. Not only do the teachers have a union attitude, many parents seem not to care about their children's education. In fact, some parents want to fight the school systems if they dare to try to establish some kind of discipline and order. But worst of all is the attitude of the children. Years ago, children grew up with "Leave it to Beaver." Today all the sitcoms aimed at the adolescent market encourage acting out as cool. Only a nerd or geek studies and makes good grades. This attitude carries over into the movies they watch and the music they listen to.

The teachers of today have themselves been taught by the same dismal failure of an educational system. Studies have shown that many teachers don't know the subject they are supposed to teach, and some can barely read or write. The schools of education they receive their degrees from are just liberal bastions of indoctrination. Forget testing the students until the teachers are required to pass a test.

Our federal government has managed to screw up the educational system terribly. But if you think about it, why should education be different from anything else they do? Abolish the Department of Education! School systems are currently given federal tax dollars based on the number of students they have in class daily. As a result, our educators are more interested in numbers than educating. The school year is longer, the days are longer, but the teaching is shorter. If our tax dollar was spent on giving a better education it might be worth it.

Unfortunately, all this money is going to pay for more and more frills, nonsense and administrators. In the past 50 years the number of administrators in schools have more than doubled for no good reason.

The schools are filled with students that have no business being there, just to run the numbers up for federal dollars. Our tax dollar should not be used to educate children whose parents are in this country illegally. You can say I am heartless, but that is what I think. I also don't want to pay to teach children to speak English or teach them their lessons in another language. If a child cannot speak English, let their parents pay the cost for them to learn it. I am also tired of paying for our schools to babysit children with such serious disabilities there is no real point in them going to school. I feel sorry for parents who have such children, but it happens. Take responsibility for your own children.

I must take the schools side on one issue. Schools are scared to death of having any form of discipline because of parents who get a lawyer and sue every time little Johnny doesn't get his way. If anyone is going to be sued it should be those parents. They should be sued because they insist on their child disrupting the system so much that other children cannot learn. We need to throw those kids out of school like they did years ago. Oh wait! I forgot that would run the numbers down for federal assistance, and it also would not be fair to little Johnny. Maybe a solution would be a separate school for children that don't conform that is run like a boot camp. But their parents should have to pay any extra costs.

Our children should be taught proper English including spelling, reading and writing. They should be taught science and mathematics. I'm talking about real science, not junk science that is just theories with no proof. They should be taught history, with an emphasis on American history. They should be taught about how American government works. And they should be taught economics. Good physical education programs should be reestablished. My tax dollar should not be wasted teaching anything else like sex education and Frisbee throwing. Only when our children understand these basics will they really be able to succeed as an adult and make an intelligent decision like how to vote.

Teachers should have exceptional pay and benefits, but only if they are exceptional teachers. We must insist on the best for the educators of our children. We should get rid of the fair to bad teachers and half of the administrators. Then take the money that was wasted on administrators and silly programs to give to the teachers. I want to see the profession of educator one that is admired and looked up to.

Unfortunately, many good teachers give up the profession because they have become as disgusted as I am with the current system. The only answer is that the people, not just parents of school aged children but all the people, DEMAND change. I am convinced that just a change in the attitude of the teachers, the parents, and the students would be all it would take to turn this situation around.

School Shootings

I had a BB gun when I was fairly young. By the time I was in my early teens I was allowed to go rabbit hunting with my father's 22 rifle. I would carry the gun through a nearby neighborhood to a store to buy the bullets. Then I would carry it through another neighborhood to a friend's house that was close to the edge of town. From there we went hunting. Nobody ever questioned my right to carry the gun. When I was in high school it was common to see rifles hanging on gun racks in the back windows of pickup trucks in the school parking lot. While guns were common in school parking lots and elsewhere, I do not remember ever hearing about a school shooting.

What happened? First, movies became more violent and graphic. Then television followed suit. Much of the music today promotes violent behavior. But worst of all are the video "games" where children become addicted to and accustomed to killing as a game and for pleasure.

Finally, the news media today tells disturbed young people that they can become famous if they just go shoot up a school. While it is the job of the media to report the news, they do not need to carry it on for days and weeks while making the shooters name and image famous.

Fools

There are many examples of people elected to office acting like fools. I could name them but you know who I am talking about. The problem is not the fool sitting in an office in D.C. The problem is the fools that vote them into office.

Of course, I guess it depends on which side you are on as to who you think is acting like a fool.

Quality

There was a large construction company I once worked for in Houston, Texas called Brown & Root. It was originally founded by a man name Herman Brown. After Herman Brown died, his younger brother, George, took over the reins of the company. By the time I started to work for them, George was an old, white-haired man. After I had worked for the company several years, I met Mr. Brown's chauffer, James, and he told me the following story.

Mr. Brown had always put in long hours. But as he got older, he had trouble keeping up. He rented a room in a downtown hotel to take a nap some afternoons because it was too far to go home to rest in the middle of the day.

The hotel needed their parking lot repaved, and the hotel manager decided to hire Brown & Root to do it as his way of showing appreciation for Mr. Brown's business. The day after the paving was finished, James took Mr. Brown to the hotel. It had been raining that day, but James could not get very close to the door. When Mr. Brown got out of the car, he stepped into a puddle. The hotel manager was at the back door waiting to greet Mr. Brown with the surprise. Before he could say anything, Mr. Brown asked him who paved the parking lot. The manager told him Brown & Root, hoping it would please him. Mr. Brown said nothing but went straight to his room and got on the phone. There was a paving crew there immediately to repave the lot. But this time without any low spots.

The point of this story is this. Even if the customer is satisfied, it is not quality if you are the one that has to step in the puddle.

Using Fear

Remember, FDR said "the only thing you have to fear, is fear itself." This was an almost prophetic utterance warning of how the Democrats would use, or misuse, fear to their advantage. The recent pandemic is a great example. I am now saying that all Americans should have a fear of the way the Democrats use fear to control Americans.

Designer Jeans

When I was young, if your jeans wore out you threw them in the rag box. Now women pay designer prices for what we used to throw away.

The New Ark

Author Unknown

In the year 2015, the Lord came unto Noah and said:

Once again the earth has become wicked and over-populated, and I see the end of all flesh before   me.

Build another Ark and save 2 of every living thing along with a few good humans. He gave Noah the blueprints, saying: You have 6 months to build the Ark before I will start the unending rain.

Six months later, the Lord looked down and saw Noah weeping in his yard - But, no Ark.

Noah! He roared, I'm about to start the rain! Where is the Ark?

Forgive me, Lord, begged Noah, things have changed.

First, I needed a building permit.

I've been arguing with the inspector about the need for a sprinkler system.

My neighbors claim that I've violated the neighborhood zoning laws by building the Ark in my yard and exceeding the height limitations.
 We had to go to the Development Appeal Board for a decision.

Then, the Department of Transportation demanded a bond be posted for the future costs of moving power lines and other overhead obstructions, to clear the passage for the Ark's move to the sea. I told them that the sea would be coming to us, but they would hear nothing of it.

Getting the wood was another problem. There's a ban on cutting local trees in order to save the spotted owl. I tried to convince the environmentalists that I needed the wood to save the owls - but no go!

When I started gathering the animals, an animal rights group sued me. They insisted that I was confining wild animal against their will. They argued that accommodations were too restrictive, and that it is cruel and inhumane to put so many animals in a confined space.

Then the EPA ruled that I couldn't build the Ark until they'd conducted an environmental impact study   on   your   proposed   flood.

I'm still trying to resolve a complaint with the Human Rights Commission on how many minorities I'm supposed to hire for my building crew.

Immigration is checking the status of most of the people who want to work.

The Trades Unions say I can't use my sons. They insist I have to hire only Union workers with   Ark-building   experience.

To make matters worse, they seized all my assets, claiming I'm trying to leave the country illegally with endangered species. So, forgive me, Lord, but it would take at least 10 years for me to finish this Ark.

Suddenly the skies cleared, the sun began to shine, and a double rainbow stretched across the sky.

Noah looked up in wonder and asked, 'You mean you're not going to destroy the world?'

"No," said the Lord.
"Your government beat me to it."

Gun Control

Any discussion of gun control must begin with the second amendment.

> "A well regulated militia being necessary to the security of a free State, the right of the People to keep and bear arms shall not be infringed."

I will be the first to admit that the way it is written is a little unclear and could be interpreted or misinterpreted in different ways. However, if you read Federalist 46 written by James Madison, it will become clear. It shows that their intent was that each citizen of this country has the right to own, and carry firearms. Other than a few activist judges with an agenda, the courts have consistently ruled this way. Gun control advocates have deliberately avoided letting their lawsuits go to the Supreme Court when possible, because they know they will lose and it will then be settled law.

So, I say to those of you who want gun control, the only way to achieve your goal is with a Constitutional amendment. But before you try it, you need to consider a few things.

First, where there is a demand for something illegal, someone will supply it. Like it or not, the bumper sticker is right. "When guns are outlawed, only outlaws will have guns." No amount of sitting in circles holding hands and chanting mantras will change that. Numerous studies have shown that where stricter gun control laws are in place, violent gun related crimes increase. In those same areas, when the gun control laws were relaxed, crime went down. The reason is very simple. Criminals are emboldened with the idea that their victims cannot protect themselves. The greater the chance their victim will protect themselves, the more reluctant the criminal is to risk his own life.

Another argument gun control advocates have is the problem of accidental shootings and killings. Some irresponsible parent leaves a loaded gun lying around, and a child gets a hold of it. I agree this is sad, and I wish it would never happen. But to say that taking away guns from everyone is the answer makes as much sense as taking everyone's car away to stop deaths caused by drunk drivers. Just as drunk drivers are punished by law, irresponsible gun owners can be punished by law.

One of the biggest reasons for the rise in gun violence in the world is the media. While Hollywood stars like George Clooney demand gun control, they themselves make their living promoting gun violence in the movies they star in. RAP music glamorizes violence. The worst culprit is video games. When our children (of any age) play realistic games of killing people they get immune to the horror of it. And some may get bored with it and feel a need to take it to a higher level. So, if you gun control advocates really want to do something to stop gun violence, change your focus to the media.

What if you got your way? What if there were suddenly no guns left in this world? Would that stop the killings? Would that stop crime? No. Next you would want to ban knives, axes, and baseball bats. The UK, which has very strict gun laws is now talking about laws to ban knives.

Auto Carpet

When I was very young all trucks and many cars had rubber on the floorboards. As time went by a very rough carpet was put in cars, then better carpet. Because the good carpet was hard to keep clean, they started putting floor mats in cars made of matching carpet that could be taken out to clean. Now they are selling rubber liners to completely cover the carpet. Next the auto companies will start selling cars with rubber on the floorboards. I guess we have come full circle.

Keeping Our Freedoms

While it is true that we should temper our speech with good common sense, that is different from someone telling us there are things we cannot say. Once we give up a little of our freedoms, we lose them all.

The War on Drugs

I do not know who first used the term "the war on drugs", but the history of our government trying to regulate and criminalize drug use began in the early 20th century. It was during the Eisenhower administration that a serious effort began to control, and hopefully stop the criminal sale and use of drugs that had harmful and detrimental effects on users and society.

There has been a growing belief that the war on drugs is unwinnable, and even possibly misguided. A growing number of people are calling for legalization of some, or even all drugs. Some states have begun to do it. I had an economics professor claim that all economists believe drugs should be legalized to produce tax revenue, even though the economics text book he used said that only a small number of economists believe so. To those who say the war on drugs is unwinnable and to those who believe everyone should be able to have access to any drug they want, I say balderdash.

The problem isn't that the war is unwinnable. The problem is we have never seriously tried to win it. The problem has always been addressed as a problem with the suppliers. The economic principle of supply and demand says that prices will go up or down based on the amount of goods in supply, and the demand of the consumer. This same principle applies here in a slightly different way. With anything illegal, it can be relied on that where there is a demand, someone will supply it. We have always worked on the belief that the suppliers are the bad guys causing all the problems, but the users are just unfortunate people that need help. But every time a supplier is eliminated, someone takes his place. We will never win the war on drugs until we crack down on demand.

Who is a drug user? When I was in my teens in the early 60's, the drugs of choice were alcohol and nicotine. The use of anything else was looked down on by the majority. By the 70's, marijuana and stronger drugs like LSD were becoming popular. Now, it is hard to find anyone under 50 who has not used illegal drugs at least once, and many who still do. The very people who are making and enforcing our drug laws are possible users.

If it is that pervasive, then it must not be all that bad, right? Why not just legalize it, and let the government tax it? -- Where do I start? -- We have enough problems with drunk drivers without adding more people driving the streets high on drugs. We have enough lost productivity caused by a myriad of other problems without adding people who are stoned. Do you really want air traffic controllers smoking pot rather than cigarettes? Do you really want people making the most important decisions of running business and government doing so with clouded minds?

I cannot take the time or space here to go into depth on all the reasons drug use is wrong. But the strongest argument I can make is to call attention to what happens with drug money. Every time someone is murdered in Mexico by the drug cartels, a drug user in the U.S. bought the bullet. Every time a US soldier is killed by the Taliban, drug sales in the U.S. contributed to buying the murder weapon. It has been shown that Al Qaeda as well as the Taliban are deeply involved in the drug trade as a source of their financing. How many other enemies of America are being financed in part by drug sales? Iran? China?

A large percent of crime is committed to support a drug habit, so the cost of crime and punishment comes out of your pocket, not the user or supplier. An argument can be made that with legalization all of these problems will go away. But at what expense, and is that completely true? Someone addicted to crack cannot hold a job. So, he will still steal to support his habit, or the government (that means you) will have to support him. If you think lung cancer caused by cigarettes is a problem you will really be unhappy with the medical problems caused by drug use, and the tax payer will pick up the costs because users will have no money or insurance. If the government regulates and taxes drugs, the cost will be added to the final sales price. That means some will still buy and sell it illegally. I give you moonshine whiskey as an example.

No, the answer is the user. Stop demand, and the supply will go away. Because it is so pervasive and goes across state lines, all illegal drug sales and use should be a federal crime. Any state law that is more lenient than federal law will be void. We need to take first time users and sentence them to a combination of treatment and punishment. They need to leave this treatment with as much support as possible, but with the full knowledge that if they get caught again, they will be facing a lengthy prison term. A third conviction means they will be removed from society for life. We should also continue to attack the suppliers. Lower-level suppliers should be sentenced to long prison terms. If it can be shown they supplied the drugs responsible for a death, it should be a capital offense. It should be assumed upper-level suppliers are responsible for at least some deaths, and therefore theirs should be considered a capital crime.

Finally, we need to stop letting state and local governments override federal drug laws by legalizing drugs that federal law declares illegal. If we want to win the war on drugs, then let's do it!!!

Taxpayer Funded Abortions

Thomas Jefferson knew a long time ago that taxpayer funded abortions was wrong. He said – "To compel a man to furnish funds for the propagation of ideas he disbelieves and abhors is sinful and tyrannical." This could also be applied to businesses funding abortions for their employees. When someone buys their products, they pay for it.

A Tale of 2 Grady's

When I was a young man, I moved to Houston, Texas. I went to work for a large company in their warehouse. The man that did the purchasing for the warehouse was a man named Grady Miller. The man that did the shipping was named Grady Fulton. Any time you went into Grady Miller's office, his desk was piled high with paperwork, and he was on the phone with some vendor. Whenever you went into Grady Fulton's office, his desk was clean and he had his feet propped up on it while he read the newspaper. It just did not seem right that Mr. Miller had to work so hard while Mr. Fulton did nothing.

Then Grady Miller went on vacation and Grady Fulton had to take his place, while still doing his own duties. Within a day, Mr. Fulton had Grady Miller's desk cleaned off and had his feet propped up reading the paper. It's not that he was not doing the job properly. On the contrary, he was taking care of everything Mr. Miller did as well as his own job.

The lesson I learned from this is that some people are just not as organized as others. There are those who work very hard only because they make their job hard.

The Bagpiper
Author Unknown

As a bagpiper, I play many gigs. Recently I was asked by a funeral director to play at a graveside service for a homeless man. He had no family or friends, so the service was to be at a pauper's cemetery in the Kentucky back-country.

I was not familiar with the backwoods, so I got lost; and being a typical man, I didn't stop for directions. I finally arrived an hour late and saw the funeral guy had evidently gone and the hearse was nowhere in sight.

There were only the diggers and crew left and they were eating lunch. I felt badly and apologized to the men for being late. I went to the side of the grave and looked down and the vault lid was already in place. I didn't know what else to do, so I just started to play.

The workers put down their lunches and began to gather around. I played out my heart and soul for this man with no family and no friends.

I played like I've never played before for this homeless man.

And as I played "Amazing Grace" the workers began to weep. They wept, I wept, we all wept together.

When I finished, I packed up my bagpipes and started for my car. Though my head hung low, my heart was full.

As I opened the door to my car, I heard one of the workers say,

"I ain't ever seen nothin' like that before, and I've been putting in septic tanks for twenty years..."

<u>Buying Votes</u>

Back in the dark ages when I was still in school, we were taught about political corruption using the example of an organization in New York political history called Tammany Hall run by a man named "Boss" Tweed. They would tax the rich, then take that money at election time to buy coal to give to the poor. Since elections were held during the cold winter months, the poor showed their appreciation by voting them back into office. Sound familiar? It sounds like the welfare programs of today! I will bet children are not taught this in public schools today, because that is exactly what the Democrats are currently doing.

<u>**Truth**</u>

Whatever happened to truth in this country? The politicians, the media, and even the schools have turned everything upside down. Now, truth is just what you want to believe, or want others to believe.

It has been said that history is written by the winners. But history is supposed to be what actually happened. What if the winners were on the wrong side? And what if those who write the history books disagree with the truth? The history of World War Two is written very differently in Japan from what we are taught in this country. Mexico sees the history of its relations with the US much differently from what we are taught. I think history should reflect the truth, the good, the bad, and the ugly. History in this country has been hijacked by the liberals. Fifty years ago, the history taught in our schools was slanted on the conservative side. It is now extremely liberal. Neither one is right. We must know and understand our history, to learn from our mistakes. Our schools have been taken over by people who believe that indoctrination into liberal thought is more important than teaching the truth. Textbooks are full if distortions, omissions, and outright untruths.

Everyone today knows and accepts that politicians lie. But rather than call it a lie, it is called spin. Politicians lie to get elected, lie to pass legislation the people won't like, and lie to get out of the messes they create. This is true of both sides. Legislative bills are even given names that are lies to fool the people. If the "Affordable Care Act" was called "Government Takeover of Medicine", more people would have been against it and fewer congressmen would have voted for it. Politicians should be held accountable for the promises they make to get elected, and their actions in office. We should not reward their lies.

The media in all its forms are biased and lie to help their side. The people of the United States deserve to know the truth. But the media believe that if they tell a lie often enough, many people will believe it. The news makes up stories and TV and the movies produce "historical" or "documentary" movies that are full of distortions and just made up "facts". Then, in cases like Al Gore and Michael Moore, they give them awards for lying. The music media also sways our youth to their way of thought. Someone in Greek history was supposed to have said something like

"I will give you a country's armies and I will take their music, and I will conquer the country."

The left tries to demonize those they disagree with. They go to great lengths to find any dirt on their opponents, and if they can't, they just make something up. By the time they are finished with someone like Donald Trump, Newt Gingrich or Sarah Palin, you would think they were the Devil himself.

There is only one, real definition for truth. And we should accept nothing less.

<u>Anchor Babies</u>

Shortly after the end of the civil war, there were those who tried to deny the freed slaves the right to vote by claiming they were not citizens. The 14th amendment to the Constitution was passed to remedy that. It said that if you are born in the USA, then you are a citizen. It was never intended to cover a pregnant woman crossing our border just in time to deliver a new American citizen.

I live right on the border with Mexico and I know what I am about to say is true. Not only do they have their babies here, they do not pay the medical bill. There are areas in southern Arizona where the hospitals do not have maternity wards because they cannot afford to take the losses. In the larger cities, the hospitals just raise the costs charged to everyone else to cover their costs.

After the child is born, it is taken back to Mexico where his or her mother applies for US welfare. The mother is free to have as many children in the US as she wants and collect welfare for all of them. Welfare checks are mailed to the mother in Mexico until each child is grown and can walk across the border as a free American citizen.

I once went to a grocery store very close to the Mexican border. Virtually every car in the lot had a license plate from Mexico. When I got to the checkout registers, EVERYONE was paying with food stamps. It is time we repealed the 14th amendment!

No Socialist Unions

Although past socialist dictatorships claimed to be for the working class; once in power they took control of production and the workers. There are no unions in socialist countries. Unions need to pay close attention to what the Democrats want to do, and vote Republican.

Free

But wait! If you buy the amazing Gizmo at the unbelievably low price of $19.95 in the next 20 minutes, we will give you a second Gizmo FREE! *Just pay separate shipping and handling.* Whatever happened to truth in advertising? There is no such thing as Free. When you agree to a second shipping charge, they double their profit.

How Much Do You Value Your Freedom?

All of the signers of the Declaration of Independence would have been hung if America had lost their war for independence. I wonder how many Americans value their freedom that much today?

Turtles and Giraffes

To be honest, the following is not mine. I heard it on TV sometime back.

Let us consider a turtle compared to a giraffe.

A giraffe, even though it is a little strange looking is a magnificent animal. A turtle, while it may be a little cute is just a turtle.

If you watch a turtle as he walks, he stops about every three feet or so and raises his head to look around. Even so, he cannot see around a bush in front of him. A giraffe on the other hand can look around and see everything for a long distance.

If, after rounding the bush, the turtle runs into a predator, all he can do is pull into his shell and hide and hope the predator is not strong enough to tear into his shell. A giraffe has few enemies willing to take him on, and those that may try will have long legs and sharp hooves to contend with.

A giraffe feeds from the tender new leaves on the top of a tree. A turtle eats bugs off the ground.

While a turtle can run surprisingly fast, a giraffe can walk faster that the turtle can run.

So, the question is, are you a giraffe or a turtle?

<u>**Paper or Plastic?**</u>

When I worked in a grocery store while in school the groceries were bagged in paper sacks. Somewhere in the late 60's or early 70's the do-gooders complained that the paper bags were responsible for too many trees being cut down. About this time the plastic industry took advantage of the situation to sell plastic bags. For a while back then when you went to the store you were asked if you wanted your groceries bagged in paper or plastic. But now the grocery stores mostly just opt for the cheaper plastic bags. Now, the do-gooders complain that plastic bags are not biodegradable and are polluting the earth. So, some stores are now using paper bags again.

This story is played over and over again by the do-gooders. They wanted hydro-electric power until they decided dams interfered with the fish. It also interferes with the natural flow of the rivers and the power lines are unsightly.

They wanted nuclear power until they discovered there was a problem with nuclear waste. Then – surprise, surprise! They now worry because nuclear power is dangerous.

They wanted ethanol, but now they are complaining that growing so much corn pollutes the waters with runoff of fertilizer and insecticides.

They wanted wind power until they found that windmills kill birds. A rich Texan named T. Boone Pickens bought into wind power and erected windmills across west Texas. He then too late discovered it was not profitable.

Obama pushed solar power by giving government money to companies building solar panels. Even with government money they went bankrupt because it is just not cost efficient.

You just can never satisfy the do-good liberals.

How Do You Dress?

I saw a woman carrying a sign in a feminist march recently that said – THE WAY I DRESS, DOES NOT MEAN YES! OK…… Then what does it mean? Let us be honest here. Both men and women dress to look good for and to attract the opposite sex. It has always been that way. I remember hot pants and halter tops in the past. I can even remember when bikini bathing suits first came out.

The fashion industry has been pushing the limits lately and the women are buying into it. They even had a fad recently called "the hooker look". Why would women allow themselves to be told by some fashion idiot in New York to show off as much of her naked body as she can get away with without being arrested, except to attract a man.

Like it or not, many men will think the way you dress means yes.

<u>Abortion</u>

In 1973, Roe vs. Wade started a war in this country. The Supreme Court of the US ruled that the states could not have a law that denied a woman the "right" to have an abortion. The ruling was based mostly on a vague interpretation of the 9th and 14th amendments which the proponents claimed gave women the right to privacy in such matters. At first the court put limitations on that "right", but subsequent rulings have pretty much eliminated all limitations.

When I say it started a war, it is because the two sides of the issue are very passionate about what they believe. For those opposed to abortion, the reason is simple. They believe the unborn child is a human life, therefore abortion is murder. Their position has been painted as a religious issue because many of the more adamant protesters make it look that way. But there are many like myself who side with their belief for other than purely religious reasons.

The arguments put forward by the pro-abortion believers are a little more complicated. The first thing you always hear is that a woman has the right to make decisions about her own body. I agree! This right has been well established for centuries. First and foremost, a woman has the right to say no. If she says no and the man still forces himself on her, that is rape. The law provides very severe penalties for rape, as it should. She can also say no with conditions. She can say no, unless the man uses a condom. Again, if a man does not abide by her wish but forces himself on her, he will be severely punished. A woman even has a right to change her mind. She may lead a man on and say yes up until the last minute. But if she then changes her mind and says no, the man better stop, no matter how he may have been led on. A woman also has a right to use whatever types of contraceptives are available to her. A woman also has the right to have whatever surgical procedures she can afford and find a doctor to perform, from having her tubes tied, to having her ovaries removed, to a complete hysterectomy if that is what she wants. But when she becomes pregnant, the question is not just her right to do whatever she wishes with her own body. If, as the anti-abortion people believe, the fetus is a human life, then there is another body other than hers to be considered that has rights also.

Another argument put forth by the pro-abortion believers is a woman's right to privacy. In fact, this is just the argument the courts first ruled on.

But, if the fetus is in fact a human life, it makes no more sense to say a woman can privately take that life than to say she can kill her husband if she does it in private.

Women have argued that by making abortion legal, they have done away with dirty back alley abortions using coat hangers. But studies have shown that many of the supposed "clinics" that now do legal abortions are not much better. Also, that argument can be used for almost anything illegal. If you make rape legal, the rapist would not have to drag their victims into the back alleys, but rather could force them to go home with him to a clean bed.

So why are groups like NOW and Planned Parenthood so adamant about this? With Planned Parenthood, it appears to be mostly just the money they make performing abortions. With NOW it is a feminist issue, so I looked at it from a feminist point of view. Suppose a man and a woman have a one-night stand, after which they each go their separate way. Aside from the possibility of contracting a disease, the man can continue on with his life without worries of consequences. But the woman can get pregnant. And if that happens, it will affect her entire life if she then gives birth to the child. The feminist cry FOUL!! It just isn't fair! Women should have the right to have irresponsible sex without consequence just like a man. So, the only answer is to have an easy way to get rid of "the problem". My response to this is that unfortunately, life is just sometimes not fair. The fact is a woman is designed to get pregnant and carry babies. It is not an acceptable option to take a human life to try to somehow equalize a woman with a man.

So, what is the answer? I believe human life should be defined as one conceived by a human male and a human female and has a heartbeat and brainwave activity. By using this definition, very early abortions could still be performed. I know this would not be acceptable to many pro-life believers, but I see it as no different than prevention using a contraceptive. Many pro-abortion believers will not like it, but no answer will satisfy everyone. I personally believe there should also be some exceptions for cases of rape, incest, and medical conditions threatening the health of the mother. But all these "solutions" are just my opinions.

The only problem will be that many will try to get around any solution. But as with any law, there are always people trying to find a way around it. There is just no easy answer.

Note: The Supreme Court has now ruled that Roe was never Constitutional. However, rather than ending the war, it has heated it up. It remains to be seen how it will end.

Stealing

When I worked for Brown & Root Inc., it was common practice that when a project was complete, if there was not another project immediately available, supervisors would be put on "standby". That meant they would continue to be paid even though there was no work for them to do. Whenever this happened, these people would often be brought into the main office to do odd jobs. I met a carpenter foreman once under just such a circumstance that told me the following story.

I don't remember his name, but he was an older gentleman that had worked for B&R for many years. He said when he was young, and just a carpenter's apprentice, he was sent with a carpenter foreman on standby to do some work at Herman Brown's house. Herman Brown was the founder of Brown and Root. He said that while they were working there, Mr. Brown came home. Apparently, the carpenter foreman saw an opportunity to make some points.

He said "Mr. Brown. Them ole boys out there at that job are stealin' from you." Mr. Brown paused for a minute, then said. "Them ole boys out there at that job are making me money.

When they stop making me money, I'll stop them from stealing."

I have encountered this attitude over and over in my business life, but only recently have I begun to really understand it. Most people will never understand what it is like to run a business worth millions, or even billions. That kind of money is beyond what most of us can comprehend. Mr. Brown was not condoning stealing. But when you are dealing at this level, sometimes it is just not worth the effort to worry about just a few thousand dollars. I sometimes still have trouble getting my head around this.

Tobacco

One of the craziest things our government does has to do with tobacco. Our Agriculture Department assists the tobacco growers just the same as any agriculture growers in this country. Then our government makes money on the sale of tobacco through taxes. Then your Health Department spends millions trying to get people to stop smoking. Go figure!

<u>**Evolution**</u>

I have always considered myself to be a logical thinker. I was raised in the Methodist church, but always seemed to have a problem with religion. It just did not pass the logical test. I had a favorite uncle that I always looked up to. When I was about 12, my brother and I visited him at college for a couple of weeks one summer. During that time, I was present when he had a conversation with some other students where he said "I find it easier to believe there either has always been a universe or it naturally evolved than to believe an all-powerful being is out there that has always been and is capable of creating the universe." That did it! My uncle could to do no wrong in my mind. So, from that point on, I was an atheist. The statement he made was so logical that I continued with these beliefs well into adulthood. However, several things have become clear to me that have changed my mind.

I think one of the greatest influences in making me believe in God is the theory of evolution. What? That sounds backwards unless you look at it logically. First, we should remember that a theory is just an idea that has not been proven as fact. And in spite of literally everyone in science believing in evolution and trying to prove it correct, no one has been able to come up with one bit of evidence that any one species has ever evolved into another species. Yes, specific species evolve into different types of the same species, but a cat has never evolved into a dog.

So why do scientists cling so to an unproven theory and treat it as fact? Science is continually proven wrong about something they swore by just the year before. This has been true throughout history. However, the scientists of today have one overriding principle – everything has a scientific explanation. And God is not a scientific option. So, until someone comes up with a better scientific theory, they will cling to evolution.

But I got away from how the theory of evolution made me believe in God. Let's look at it logically with an example of a plant. There is a very large plant, somewhere in the area of Borneo or Indonesia I believe, that is blood red in color, smells like rotting flesh, and consumes insects that are attracted to it. The scientists say this is a great example of evolution. But for that to be so, the plant's relatives in the past would have to been able to see to know what color to evolve into. It would need to have been able to smell to know what odor to mimic. It would have to have the intelligence to understand that to make the changes would attract insects and have the ability to make the decision to change itself. But most importantly, since evolution is supposed to happen gradually over time, it would have to be able to communicate to its offspring to continue with the effort to change. No, logically the only answer is the plant is just what it was created to be.

In the animal world the scientists say that some species like the crocodile have not changed in millions of years. If the idea of evolution is species continue to evolve and change for the better, why has the crocodile not evolved? Is it already perfect? If not, then why would the crocodile not evolve into a horse like an ape supposedly evolved into a man? This brings up another question. Why do we still have apes? Should not they have evolved too?

Some years back our government, in its wisdom, decided it was their duty to mandate fuel efficiency in automobiles. One way to improve efficiency is through aerodynamics. The problem is that there is only one aerodynamically perfect design. As a result, for many years it was hard to distinguish between automobile makes except by their emblem. Evolution is the same. If the purpose of evolution is to evolve towards perfection, why is it that every form of life on earth is not at least very similar? Why did man evolve into an intelligent being, but a worm is still a worm? Why did some fish grow legs and move on land to evolve into a higher life form while other fish are still just fish? Why did some species evolve in a manner that makes them totally dependent on another species? For example, did an apple tree evolve to be dependent on a honey bee to be able to reproduce because that is the logical way it should evolve according to the theory of evolution? How did plants reproduce before they became dependent on insects to pollinate them? Again, no, no, no! Logically, none of this makes sense! The only logical answer is, once again, everything is as it was created to be.

For anyone who considers it logically, evolution just does not hold up. I choose to believe God is the only logical answer, but everyone is free to believe what they wish. As long as you don't try to push your beliefs on me! And evolution <u>IS</u> a religious belief as much as atheism is. I think whatever you decide to believe is between you and God

Liver

As I said in the previous story, a butcher I worked with named Bob Nolan and I became close friends. That was a little strange because Bob was at least in his 50's, and I was just in my teens. But Bob seemed to take an interest in me, and whenever I had a little spare time, I would go back to the meat department and talk to him.

One day I stopped by to talk, and Bob had a huge cow's liver on his block cutting it up. Back in those days they used wax covered cardboard cups to hold such things. Bob had maybe a dozen of these containers on the left side of his work, and maybe a dozen more on the right. As he cut the liver, he would put every other slice in a container on the right or left. This looked strange, and my curiosity got the best of me so I asked Bob why he was doing that.

Bob widened the smile he always had and said, "the containers on this side are cow's liver, and the ones on that side are calves' liver." Wait a minute! I protested. They are all being cut from the same liver. Bob just smiled and explained. "They don't butcher calves, but some people still insist on getting calves liver. So, I give them what they want, and they swear it is better than the cow's liver."

Cell Phones

If evolution is true, humans in the not-too-distant future will be born with cell phones in their ears. Don't get me wrong. I think having a telephone that I can carry with me is a great invention. But too many people today are hooked on cell phones like it was heroin. Our youth literally could not function without them. I have seen kids in my neighborhood texting each other when they are just feet apart. I guess that saves them the effort of talking. In the past, if you were away from home, people would just have to leave a message and you would get back to them. I can remember when you could not even leave a message. While it is nice to be able to call home when you need to know what your wife needs at the market, we lived perfectly well without it. It is great to be able to receive emergency calls wherever you may be, but to take a non-emergency call while in a live conversation with someone else is just rude.

Lawyers and Justice

You have heard it said that in this country everyone is innocent until proven guilty. But that is not true. If the person did, in fact commit the crime, then he or she is guilty. But our system of justice "presumes" innocence until the courts find the person guilty. There is a very good reason for this, and it is not one I disagree with. As I have previously said, I do not trust government. And you cannot trust human nature in such matters. Any other system would allow for too many people to be convicted of crimes because someone was mistaken, or someone did not like the person, or the government wanted to silence someone.

The main problem with our system of justice in this country is it has been ruined by the lawyers.

jus·tice
noun \\'jəs -təs\\
1 a : the maintenance or administration of what is just especially by the impartial adjustment of conflicting claims or the assignment of merited rewards or punishments b : JUDGE c : the administration of LAW; especially : the establishment or determination of rights

according to the rules of law or EQUITY 2 a : the quality of being just, impartial, or fair b (1) : the principle or ideal of just dealing or right action
 (2): conformity to this principle or ideal: RIGHTEOUSNESS c: the QUALITY of conforming to law

Let us look at criminal justice first. We no longer have a criminal justice system. We now have something like a ball game played with four pieces – the prosecution (the home team), the defense (the visiting team), the judge (the referee), and the jury (the scorekeeper). And like so much else in America these days, who wins this game is often rigged.

Prosecutors are supposed to be the good guys. They are supposed to represent "the people." And, to be fair, most of them do just that. But there are several problems. Prosecutors are lawyers, and too often they are the ones who are just not good enough to make a living as a defense attorney. So "the people" are often at a disadvantage. The rights of the accused are numerous and well established. If the prosecutor makes one mistake, the guilty often go free. If the defense makes a mistake, the defendant can appeal any conviction. I am not saying the rights of the accused should be changed. It would just be nice if we had more competent prosecutors sometimes.

Another problem with prosecutors is the job can be highly political. There are too many times a prosecutor uses his job for political gain. It is OK I guess when someone like Rudy Giuliani profits politically from prosecuting a legitimate case against organized crime. Too often, however, we have cases like that jerk prosecutor in the Duke Lacrosse case. He brought charges against a group of young men that he either knew, or should have known were innocent, just for political gain. A previous attorney general, Janet Reno, before she became the attorney general, prosecuted a child molestation case in Florida against innocent individuals for political gain. There was also a famous case in Austin, Texas where a prosecutor named Ronnie Earl spent his entire career prosecuting people he disagreed with politically. Something should be done to take all politics out of prosecution.

The defense lawyers are seen as the bad guys. That is, of course, unless you are the one accused of a crime. They are seen as the guys that want criminals set free, not punished. This perception is fueled by the high-profile lawyers we see on

TV during famous cases. The truth is, many are honest men just trying to do their job of protecting their client's rights to a fair trial. I have no problem with that. I do have a problem with the fact that the real money for a defense lawyer is in having the ability to get a guilty person off scot free. The better a lawyer proves himself able to use whatever tricks or other means he can get away with to get his client off, the more money he can command for his services. So, we have a system where people with money get more "justice" than those who don't. Just look at the "dream team" in the O.J. trial for a good example. Even lower paid attorneys in cases like the Casey Anthony trial do it because they are trying to build their reputation so they can charge more. A defendant SHOULD have his rights to a fair trial protected. But that does not mean his lawyer has the right to use every trick available to turn a criminal loose on society again.

Judges are the referees in this game. They are supposed to be there to insure neither the prosecution nor the defense gets away with bending the rules. Most of them do a good job. Unfortunately, too many are either not competent, too political, or just make rulings on personal opinions not backed up in the law.

There needs to be a better system of removing bad judges. But there needs to be protections in place to be sure a judge is not removed for political reasons.

The jury is the scorekeeper. It is their job to decide who won the game. I have served on several juries in my life and believe in the system. I believe most jurors take their job very seriously. It is easy to condemn them for a ruling like the one in the Casey Anthony trial, but in truth, they took their job seriously and ruled that even though the accused may very well have been guilty, the prosecution did not prove it. The two biggest problems with juries are that too many people try to get out of jury service, and you have the occasional idiot chosen to sit on a jury. In cases like the O.J. trial, the entire panel were idiots. You also have the problem of the way jurors are screened by the lawyers that allows either side to attempt to stack the jury in their favor.

Crime and punishment should not be a game!

The next area we need to look at in which lawyers are involved is in the civil and business arena. In my opinion this is where they have really gummed up the works. This is also a game, but I will illustrate it as a war game. There are three sides at war here. Business, the lawyers, and the people. It is so complicated it is often difficult to see who is winning. But I guarantee the lawyers will not lose.

With businesses the lawyers attack from two sides in a manner that ensures they all succeed. One front is comprised of a group of lawyers that attack the business, the other front is those who profit from the first attack by representing the business. Businesses today MUST have a good team of lawyers to protect them from… the other lawyers. Much of the cost of business today is in the cost of defending lawsuits and paying lawyers to tell them how to run their business without being sued. Even the businesses insurance company tells them what they must do to keep their insurance because the lawyers for the insurance look at the risks. While all these lawyers get rich, the business passes on the cost of their legal expenses, their insurance, and anything paid in lost lawsuits to you. Yes, YOU pay for it all. In this war game, the consumer is the innocent civilian being bombed in Dresden. So, the lawyers win this battle, the businesses lick their wounds, and the people lose.

If you watch any television at all you have seen advertisements for law firms telling you if you ever did this or that, you have a right to compensation. In the war game, these lawyers are like black marketers getting filthy rich on the spoils of war by taking advantage of a businesses exposed flanks. Sometimes there is a legitimate basis for a claim, but too many times it is more than a little questionable. However, the lawyers on both sides know that the issues are too complicated for the average juror to understand. And because the media has painted "big business" as the bad guy for so long, they know the jurors are more likely to find against the business. So, the business realizes that to fight this battle would mean paying their lawyers millions to defend a case they will probably loose and have to pay millions more in claims. So, it is easier and cheaper to call for a cease fire and just negotiate a settlement. Besides, they can pass the cost on to you. So, the black-market lawyers get rich, their clients get a small negotiated settlement, the business has another wound to lick, and the people get screwed once again.

Finally, after the lawyers have turned all the criminals loose and ruined as many businesses as possible, they turn to the average citizen. They have convinced Americans it is their right, if not their duty, to sue each other whenever something happens you are not happy about. After all, nobody is really hurt, their insurance pays for it. No. Everybody pays for it in higher insurance premiums. Only the lawyers come out ahead.

I am tired of playing legal games where the rules guarantee I will lose. I am certainly not qualified to tell anyone how to resolve this. But I believe a good start would be tort reform. The problem is the politicians are mostly lawyers themselves, and they have been bought and paid for by other lawyers. When we get our political problems corrected, only then can we hope to get the lawyers reined in.

__The W Word__

A while back there was a TV show called "The Whitest Kid I Know." (Or something like that.) I never watched the program, but it was my understanding that what is meant by this title is that to be white is not cool. And the implication is that the "whiter" you are, the worse it is. If the word white is now a racial slur, shouldn't we be saying "the W word?" And shouldn't the producers of that show be forced to go to sensitivity training?

Also – Back in the 70's it was common to refer to your male friends as boy when addressing them. Nothing was meant by it. It was similar to women today referring to their friends as girl. But black men took great exception to it. I had a very good friend back then who was black, and if I ever referred to him as boy he said – "What do you mean boy?!! Do you call an alligator a lizard?"

Lately I have heard a lot of black people referring to "white boys". I want to say back to them - "What do you mean boy?!! Do you call an alligator a lizard?"

State's Rights

The term "States Rights" is treated like it was some kind of curse word these days. It started being treated that way when the southern states used it to defend their segregation policies. But just because they were wrong on that issue, does not detract from the truth. State's rights are guaranteed by the Constitution in the tenth amendment.

The powers not delegated to the United States by the Constitution, nor prohibited by it to the States, are reserved to the States respectively, or to the people.

The signers of the constitution wanted to be sure the federal government was limited in its power. This amendment clearly does that. The liberals today want the federal government to have almost limitless power, therefore must do something to do away with or at least minimize this amendment. So, they have demonized the term "state's rights." Now, because the people – the states – have little by little given up their rights under this amendment, they have allowed the federal government to put their tentacles into much more than they have a constitutional right to. Nowhere in the constitution does the federal government have the authority to get involved the way they have with welfare, labor, education, and numerous other areas.

State's rights is a fact. It is a constitutional right. One that the states need to take back!

History

George Orwell has been quoted as saying, "To be converted (to socialism) you have to destroy your past, destroy your history. You have to stamp on it, you have to say 'my ancestral culture does not exist, it doesn't matter."

A country is defined by its history, both good and bad. To replace our country with a socialist country, they must tear down our history first. That is what is currently happening and it must be stopped!

<u>The EPA</u>

Every now and then a movement or group become so powerful, they are able to get a department of the US government dedicated to their cause. The Labor Department is a good example. It was formed when unions were powerful in this country, and still exists way past its usefulness. Several years ago, the environmental movement in this country had a large enough following to get the Environmental Protection Agency formed. If there ever was a government agency that should have never existed, it is the EPA.

First, let me assure you I am an environmentalist. But unlike many environmentalists, I think I have good sense. I love going to the mountains, to our parks, to go fishing, etc. I hate to see trash and destruction in our country's pristine areas. I believe our government should use some common-sense methods to control this. But it can be done with existing laws and under the Interior Department, not an entire government agency.

First, Congress gave the EPA the ability to more or less make up their own rules as they go along.

Then, what has happened over the years is the EPA has been taken over by some environmentalist nuts that are more interested in protecting a bug than what is good for society as a whole. They have made it so hard to comply with their regulations, the price of everything goes up.

I think we should drill for oil in Anwar, off the eastern seaboard, in Montana or anywhere else we can find oil. There are enough regulations and oversight to make it safe. We need to mine coal and any other natural resources we need. Mother earth is not going to be destroyed, or even shed a tear if we are smart. We need to use common sense with emission controls and quit listening to the prophets of doom who only want to scare people so they can make a profit.

Note: Here again a recent Supreme Court ruling has reigned in the power of the EPA to arbitrarily make rules. Thank you, Donald Trump for putting justices on the court that understand the Constitution.

Confused?

Homosexuals have always been prevalent in the entertainment industry. That part of their character makes them good at their trade and I do not have a problem with that. But they used to try to hide it. Women used to swoon over Rock Hudson, but they had no idea he wasn't interested in any woman. Now you see characters in movies and TV that are supposed to be some kind of ladies' man but are openly effeminate. In fact, all television sitcoms seem to be like that. This has to confuse young people growing up.

Note: Here again the nuts are taking over the asylum. Recently, the homosexuals have taken over education and the entertainment industry completely so that almost all children's books and movies promote their values. We have even lost Walt Disney, of all companies. Walt must be turning over in his grave.

Gambling and Taxes

Nevada had a problem. Their population was very small. There was not much land good for farming or anything else. There was very little to attract tourists, and there were not any major cross roads or through highways in the state. Nevada needed a gimmick to attract people and raise revenue. So, Nevada legalized gambling. It worked, but it attracted criminal elements and other problems. After many years Nevada has managed to get control of much (not all) of the organized crime aspect, but still has many other problems.

Some years back, other states began to have fiscal problems caused by out-of-control spending and looked to Nevada as an example of a way to raise new revenues. One by one, many states legalized at least some form of gambling or started state lotteries. Then the Indians got onto the act and started opening casinos to raise money. I know many of you see no problem with a little innocent gambling as a form of recreation. But we need to consider why it was illegal for so many years.

Many people, not all but many, get addicted to gambling. These people will gamble away their entire paychecks. Some will steal or embezzle to raise gambling money. Many children go without necessities because their parents have gambled away all the family income. Numerous studies have shown the cost in crime and welfare is higher than the income the state receives in taxes. This is especially true of casinos on Indian reservations where the states receive no taxes but must pay for all the problems created.

Other studies have shown that most lottery winners blow all the money within a few years and end up broke again. The lottery just finances one big temporary party for the winner. Few end up better off in the long run.

Only the people owning the gambling establishments come out ahead. While it may be just innocent entertainment to some people, we need to consider if we really want our government, in any form, profiting from the addictions and misery of others. We need to do away with all government sponsored gambling. It would be better to just cut back on spending so the governments did not need the extra revenue. Those of you who want to gamble can go to Nevada like it used to be.

Quotas and Affirmative Action

Your government, in its infinite wisdom, decided it could right every wrong that ever happened to minorities by just making sure everything represented the right percentages. If, for instance, 12% of the population was of African descent, then 12% of every opportunity should be given to them. But I said that incorrectly. It was not just the opportunity. They got it no matter what. Twelve percent of all police officers had to be black, even if they were less qualified. Twelve percent of all fire fighters had to be black, even if they were less qualified. As a result, Americans are being protected by people who may not be the best qualified. In some cases, they may not be qualified at all. Qualified people are passed over and jobs or promotions given to less qualified. This has become known as reverse discrimination. But those given the preferential treatment do not want to hear about it. They think it is OK to discriminate now to correct a past discrimination.

Our colleges and universities love the quota system. While many students must meet certain standards to be admitted, others are given a pass. Then they are allowed to skate by and get their degrees when some can barely read and write.

Then they take that degree and get a job teaching your children. Or even possibly, become president of the United States.

I say, if you must have a quota system, it must be administered fairly across the board. From now on, only 12% of all pro basketball players may be black. Wait a minute!! You say the quality of players and the game will go down? My answer is this. Is basketball more important than police protection?

Right now, you are thinking I am a prejudiced, racist bigot. What I am is tired. I am tired of all this nonsense. We are all Americans. Give everyone equal opportunity according to their abilities. If you are not qualified, study harder, work harder, do your best, then accept what you can qualify for. If you are truly denied equal opportunity, then you deserve to have help. But that help should be through the courts, not a law giving everyone of a certain group preferential treatment. If not, quit beefing about not having it as good as the next guy.

Mascots

A few years back, New Mexico State University named a new Chancellor. One of the first things she did was to do away with the school mascot. Their mascot for many years was Pistol Pete, a cowboy image with guns drawn and firing. But guns were unacceptable to the new Chancellor. I don't know what they did to replace him, but may I suggest that since it is a primarily agricultural school, they could call themselves the "Farmers" and have Mr. Green Jeans as their mascot.

What if this way of thinking was taken to every college or University? Just south of NMSU is UT El Paso. They are the Miners and have a mascot of a prospector with a pick over his shoulder. A PICK!! That won't do! Change their mascot from a miner to a minor and have the mascot a cherub faced child. Notre Dame could change from the Fighting Irish to the Sweet Little Leprechauns. USC Trojans could keep their name but change the mascot from a Greek warrior to a condom. Texas could change from the Longhorns to the Milk Cows. The Wyoming Cowboys could be the Sheep Herders. The Georgia Bulldogs could be the Poodles. The Texas Tech Red Raiders could be the Pink

Ladies. The possibilities are endless. And just think of what you could do with professional sports mascots! (*Since I first wrote this some professional teams have gone nuts!*)

Fortunately, the alumni at NMSU forced the new chancellor to change her ruling on their mascot.

Flood Insurance

Insurance companies may be bad in many ways, but they are not stupid. In the past, they refused to insure properties on the coast that were subject to storm damage like hurricanes, and properties on river banks that flooded periodically. So, our government established the federal flood insurance program. Because people could now build right on the beach or river bank, land values skyrocketed. Now, only the rich can afford to build in these places, and they often build very expensive homes. When the inevitable happens and they get flooded or blown away every five to ten years, the federal government rebuilds their house and buys them all new furniture. The insurance companies may not be stupid, but your government is. And you are paying the bill.

Labels

Has anyone else other than me noticed that almost all labels on products you buy have changed to include Spanish as well as English? Because we have looked the other way while millions of Spanish speaking individuals entered our country illegally, businesses now feel obligated to communicate with them in their native language. I say if they are going to live here, even illegally, let them learn English.

Out of State Money

We need a Constitutional Amendment that outlaws out of state and out of district contributions to political campaigns. That would shut down people like George Soros from buying elections.

The Palestinians

After World War II, the Europeans and Americans had a collective guilty conscience about what Hitler had done to the Jews. What had happened shocked the civilized world. We should have, and could have done something earlier, but there were those who decided it best to look the other way. After the war, many people of the Jewish faith wanted to return to their ancestral homeland to start a country of their own. There was one problem with that. Their ancestral homeland had been occupied by other people for almost 2000 years.

The Romans got fed up with the problems the Jews were causing them, and in the first century AD they attacked Judea and fought several successive wars. They killed many of the Jews and the rest were sold into slavery or scattered. The area once known as Judea became a land occupied by the Samaritans and other Semites living in the area. Over the centuries names and borders changed until a country called Palestine was formed after World War I. Although the new borders were defined by a treaty between France and England, the people had lived there for centuries. So, when the Jews wanted to make a new state called Israel in their ancestral homeland, they had to take it from the Palestinians.

I believe Israel has the right to exist as a country for just the same reasons every other country has that right. Every country in the world today has a history of wars where one people were conquered by another. The United States took this land from the natives that lived here, then rebelled against English rule. Most people in Briton are decedents of Norse, Saxon and Norman invaders. Boundaries are defined by conquerors. But usually, the conquered and the conquerors then live together in relative peace. The problem with Israel is it is a country based on a common heritage and religion. As such, the prior inhabitants do not fit in. While not necessarily required to, most Palestinians decided to leave the area. But they have always felt their homeland was stolen from them. To make things worse, none of the neighboring countries wanted them. There were tens of thousands of people with no place to go and no way to support themselves.

The Israelis saw it the same as themselves. All the surrounding countries share the same common heritage and religion with the Palestinians. They said let them take them in. But the surrounding countries have problems enough of their own. Every country in the Middle East sees it as a problem that would be easily resolved if the Jews would just go away and let the Palestinians go home. They also identify with their fellow Muslims. So, we have this problem that now exists, and there is no easy answer to it.

Europe and the US have backed Israel from the beginning, again mostly because they felt guilty. I see few if any other instances where we put such effort and finances into a small country that has no real significance otherwise. Our national interest would be better served with peace in the area. Much of the terrorism in the world today can be traced to the problem. However, I am not advocating we change our position. Israel is a fact, and everyone will have to come to terms with that. They have also, for the most part, been loyal allies and friends to the US. We cannot and must not turn our backs on Israel. But we, as civilized human beings cannot and must not turn our backs on a people that have been left homeless for more than 50 years.

What is the answer? First, the US needs to use its power and influence to bully both sides into working together for a solution. We have put up with this nonsense for way too long. The Palestinians deserve a home of their own, but cannot return to the previous country of Palestine. If they would agree to stop all terrorism and other militant acts against Israel and elsewhere, I think all parties involved including the US, Europe, Israel, the Arabs, and the other Muslim countries could carve out a country somewhere. The amount of money now being wasted fighting could be better spent establishing a Palestinian homeland. If we do not do something like this very soon, I fear this will end up very badly for everyone.

Gas Prices

You often hear people complain about the high price of gasoline, and the obscene profits the oil companies make. OK, let us compare the price of gasoline to a similarly priced liquid, milk. The oil companies spend millions locating and drilling for oil. Even when they find an area they think is promising, they sometimes spend millions drilling dry wells. Since it is often overseas or under the seas, they spend millions getting the oil to the surface, and then shipping it to the US. Once here, the oil companies have spent millions building refineries, and millions more operating them. Once the oil is refined into gasoline it is sent through pipelines that cost millions, and then trucked to the stations. Then there is the cost to build and run the stations.

Dairy farmers on the other hand have cows that are fed by green grass and hay. The farmer has the expense of milking machines and pasteurizing. It then has to be bottled and refrigerated before it is trucked to a separately owned grocery store. In the end, they both cost about the same.

Now, try comparing the cost of that little bottle of water you drink to the price of gasoline.

__The Bomb__

I am getting tired of everyone wanting the US to apologize to Japan for dropping the bomb. We developed the atomic bomb because Germany was working on one and we knew we had to beat them to it or we would lose the war. When the Germans realized they would lose before they could develop one, they tried to send their research and designs to Japan. Fortunately, the submarine carrying the plans was sunk before it got to Japan. But if Japan developed it first, they would have used it against us.

Truman knew that by dropping the bomb, he would actually save hundreds of thousands of American _and_ Japanese lives that would have been lost had we invaded the Japanese homeland.

Japan has never apologized for the sneak attack on Pearl Harbor, the Bataan death march, or any of their many other atrocities. Research what they did at Nanking, China. We should never apologize for doing what was right. NEVER!

The Two Party System

I am a firm believer in the 2-party system. Yes, I know there is a Libertarian Party, a Green Party, and even a Communist Party that run candidates in most elections. But the two main parties are still the dominate ones. In other countries where parliamentary systems of government are established, there are usually numerous parties. This results in collaborative governments where parties cooperate for mutual benefit. But the coalitions are fragile and often fall apart. Countries like Italy have not had a functioning government in years.

Even though I like the system, I don't like what the parties have become. It is one thing to have a group of likeminded people working together for a goal of what is thought to be good for the country. It is another thing to make the party more important than the country. Both parties do this. Both parties are corrupt. Unfortunately, the Democrats have become experts in corruption, while the Republicans have remained pretty inept in it. Because the corruption is so obvious, many have left both parties and become "Independents". Others rally behind one party or the other but try to force them into their way of thinking. Both of these cause problems.

Independents are the worse problem. They tend to vote either way based on emotions. They are what is often referred to as the swing vote. They are also allowed to vote in primaries (which I think is wrong) and dilute the vote of the true believers on either side. I believe the independents are the cause of the poor candidates the Republicans seem to nominate so often. People who call themselves independent need to get off the fence and make up their mind what they believe. Being afraid to take a stand is not an admirable trait.

You also have the problem of when a President is running unopposed in their own party for reelection. Currently, the Democrats are free to vote in the Republican primaries for the candidate they believe is most easily defeated. The primary system should be done away with and go back to the conventions nominating a candidate, or there needs to be a way of guaranteeing the purity of the primary vote.

The Democrat party is a coalition of groups, mostly far left. Feminists, Hispanics, unions, Jewish, ACLU, environmentalists, socialists and other racial and radical groups are the Democratic party. There are so many radical groups in the Democratic fold, the party has trouble pleasing them all. Some are so radical it would be political suicide to push their agenda, so the Democrats voice support but do nothing to promote their agenda blaming the Republicans for their inability to do anything.

The Republican voters generally consist of center to far right-minded people. They tend to believe in American exceptionalism. They are mostly capitalists, Christians, and generally believe in old style values. They believe in a strong national defense and protecting our borders. While some may consider the Tea Party to be extreme, they will mostly agree with the Tea Party's stand on fiscal conservatism. Unlike the Democrats, the Republicans have trouble holding their groups together. Republicans tend to be idealists who often bicker amongst themselves.

It is easy to get disgusted with both parties and want to form a third party. But third parties just split the vote on either side and guarantee the other party's candidate will win. As much as Ross Perot tries to deny it, he singlehandedly is responsible for the election of Bill Clinton. Twice!

The Republicans have been portrayed as the party of big business, but many business leaders put their money in the Democratic coffers. There are just as many rich Democrats as there are rich Republicans. Both parties cater to the rich and big business to get their financial support. While Democrats decry the rich for not paying their fair share, everyone in the affluent community knows it is just talk to get the votes of the poor. There are always tax loopholes and overseas banks to protect their money.

It has now reached the point where a party (the Democrats) thinks they can openly commit voter fraud. They seem to believe that their hold on power is the most important thing.

The answer is for the American people to take back their government by getting control of the corruption on both sides. The two-party system can work well if controlled.

Foreign Aid

One of the basic concepts of liberal thought is that it is the duty of those who have the most to help those that are less fortunate. We are currently in a debate about whether the "rich" in this country should pay more taxes. The entire concept of foreign aid is basically the same.

While I have no problem helping others in need when you can, we as a country need to look at our foreign aid policy again. It is just another form of welfare. Those who receive it begin to take it for granted and look on it as deserved. Not only is there no gratitude, it inhibits the desire and need to improve themselves. There are other forms of help we can give that are much better than cash.

As hard hearted as it may sound, we need to make foreign aid decisions based on what is the most beneficial for our country. We need to stop pouring money into countries with corrupt governments that just pocket the money or use it to control their citizens. If a corrupt government is one that is better than the alternative, we need to tie any aid to proven changes to better the country. Countries that have proven to be good friends and allies should come first. Other aid should be based solely on if the benefits we receive at least equal the outlay.

We should not send one dime overseas until everyone that needs help in this country has received help. It makes no sense to help people in other parts of the world when we have our own citizens in need. This includes spending money for military actions in other countries because someone believes their people are oppressed. Just think of all the good that could have been done in the US with the money we recently wasted in Libya.

I believe that in the long run, most foreign aid hurts our relations with the countries we try to help. They resent what we have, and think we are patronizing them. They take our money but will turn on us as soon as it is in their interest to do so. It is a mistake to think we can buy friends.

Singers / Actors

Why is it everyone seems to think a movie star or famous singer is somehow more intelligent that the average citizen? Everyone from Congress to the morning shows wants their opinion on everything. There is no reason to believe someone like Whoopie Goldberg knows any more about a subject than the average Joe on the street. In fact, in many cases there is good reason to believe they don't know Jack. So, spare me the lectures. Just shut up and sing (or act).

A House Divided

The Bible says a house divided against itself cannot stand. That is true no matter your religious beliefs. That is why the Socialist Democrats are working so hard to divide Americans.

Accident Report
Author Unknown

Sir,

I am writing in response to your request for additional information on the accident I had on the job. In block number 3 of the accident report form I put "trying to do a job alone" as the cause of my accident. In your letter, you requested that I explain more fully. I trust that the following will be sufficient.

I am a bricklayer by trade. On the day of the accident, I was working late on the roof of a new 6 story building. When I completed my work, I found that I had about 500 pounds of brick left over. There was no one left on the job to help, and rather than carry the bricks down by hand, I decided to lower them in a barrel using a pulley which fortunately was attached to the side of the building at the sixth floor.

I swung the barrel out and loaded the brick into it. Then I went down to the ground level and untied the rope, being sure to hold tight to the rope to assure a slow decent of the brick. You will note in block 11 of the report that I weigh approximately 185 pounds.

Due to my surprise at being jerked off the ground so suddenly, I lost my presence of mind and forgot to let go of the rope. Needless to say, I proceeded up the side of the building at a rather rapid rate.

In the vicinity of the third floor, I met the barrel coming down. This explains the fractured skull and broken collarbone. Slowed only slightly, I continued my rapid ascent, not stopping until the fingers of my right hand were two knuckles deep into the pulley.

Fortunately, by this time I had regained my presence of mind and held onto the rope in spite of my pain. At approximately the same time however, the barrel of bricks hit the ground and the bottom came out of the barrel. Devoid of the weight of the bricks, the barrel now weighed approximately 50 pounds. I refer you again to my weight shown in block 11.

As you can imagine I began a rapid decent down the side of the building. In the vicinity of the third floor, I met the barrel coming up. This accounts for the two fractured ankles and the lacerations of my legs and lower body. The encounter with the barrel slowed my decent enough to lessen my injuries when I hit the pile of bricks to only three fractured vertebrae.

I am sorry to report, however, that as I lay there on the bricks in pain watching the barrel hanging six stories above me, I again lost my presence of mind and let go of the rope.

I hope this answers all your questions concerning my accident. Should you have any further questions you may contact me here at the hospital as I am told I will be here for quite some time.

Reminds me of how some politicians are running our country!

Communism in the Americas

While most countries in North and South Americas other than Canada and the US have always been what was once called third world, and many have been dictatorships, we have had little problems with communism or other outside influences until recently. In 1823, US President Monroe declared what became known as the Monroe doctrine. It basically put the rest of the world on notice that the US would consider any attempts of foreign powers to take over a country in the Americas an act of war against the US. It actually worked very well up until liberal thought took hold in the US in the 20th century. While liberals may not have all believed in communism, their socialist leanings were closer to them than the capitalists. They thought the US should not support any dictatorship, even if the replacement government was communist and supported by foreign governments.

Cuba was the first. Fidel Castro fought to overthrow a dictatorship there, and many in the US supported him even though no one really knew what kind of government he would form if he won. Castro, like many before and after him, hid his political leanings until he gained power. When he created a communist government with the help of the USSR, he broke the Monroe doctrine. When the US did nothing, the Monroe doctrine effectively no longer existed.

We have tolerated Cuba since then with varying degrees of ups and downs. But they were the only communist country in the Americas until Nicaragua elected a man named Daniel Ortega who declared his country communist after elected. Jimmy Carter was there and enthusiastically declared them the winners of the election. While Carter and the liberals in the US almost welcomed him with open arms, President Reagan worked to undo the damage. The communists were not able to gain enough power before the next election and were voted back out. (Ortega has since regained power but has learned his lesson and has somewhat downplayed his political leanings.)

Communism, a form of socialism, depends on the ignorance and dissatisfaction of the people. In third world countries, it is easy for communists to take over if there is either a weak dictatorship, or a democracy where the government allows the wealthy few to dominate the poor masses. Central and South America have been ripe for communist takeover for years. Our government has supported dictators and corrupt governments there because they were considered the best option at the time. But that was a big mistake.

In 1998, Hugo Chavez was elected president of Venezuela. Through the support of the poor and manipulations of the law and constitution he managed to make himself a virtual communist dictator. While he periodically ran for reelection, he had gained control of the process in a way to insure his reelection. Since then, with the help of Chavez and Cuba, several other South American countries have been taken over by communists or extreme socialists. All these countries have openly defied and criticized the US. Chavez has since died, but his party continues to control the country. It is on the verge of total ruin and collapse.

There are liberals in the US like actor Sean Penn who see all this as a positive change. Even President Obama cordially greeted Chavez in meetings and vowed to give US aid and support to other socialist countries in the region. While I am not advocating that we send troops to overthrow any regime, we need to make it very clear we do not support them. We need to cut off aid to these countries and we need to seize the US assets of Citgo, the Venezuelan Oil

Company, to pay back the US companies that had their assets seized and nationalized by Chavez. Then we need to put a high tariff on Venezuelan oil and other goods coming from the region. We need to work to restore democracy in these countries, then we should do all we can to improve conditions so they will not turn to these people again.

Gun Buy Backs

"Participating in a gun buy-back program because you think criminals have too many guns is like having yourself castrated because you think your neighbors have too many kids."

Clint Eastwood

1984 Revisited

In 1949 a book was published that was written by a man using the pen name George Orwell. The title of the book was 1984. It was a fictional novel about what the world would be like in the year 1984. In the book, the world was a horrific place where the government brutally controlled all aspects of life. I read the book many years ago. It was tortuous reading on the one hand, but on the other hand, I could not put the book down. About the same time, I saw a movie made from the book. For a long time, there was much talk and even anxiety about how much, if any of his predictions would come true. Then the year 1984 came and went. There was a collective sigh of relief that Orwell was wrong. But was he? Let us compare his predictions to what has changed since his time.

In the book the world was divided into only 3 countries. At any given time, two of the countries were allied in war against the other, but the alliances often changed. **Reality.** After World War II the world was divided into 3 parts – the free world, the communist world, and the third world. At any given time, the third world countries would ally with either of the other two based on what was in their best interest. While there was not always a fighting war, we were continually in what was referred to as the cold war. You do not hear much about this since the fall of the USSR, but it is still pretty much true.

The story is about a man living in one of the three countries. There are signs everywhere warning the people that Big Brother is watching them. In fact, there are cameras everywhere watching people. Each person had a television in their house that could not be turned off and that ran government propaganda continuously. It also had a camera in it watching everything going on in every house. **Reality.** Until several years back, all the 24 hour news channels pretty much ran what the democratic party's propaganda people put out. While you could turn it off, there was no other "news" available. In most countries today, there are cameras everywhere watching what is happening. While most are not run by the government, they have access to any of them when they want to see what is happening. There are also satellites capable of watching anything that is happening anywhere in the world. I recently met a young woman that had grown up in communist East Germany. She said that after the fall of the communist government there, it was discovered that many of the homes had hidden cameras installed.

In the story, the government is divided into four ministries. The Ministry of Truth is the government propaganda machine that publishes all the lies the government wants the people to believe. The Ministry of Love is the police that brutally enforce the government regulations with torture and murder. The Ministry of Peace is the war department. And the Ministry of Plenty is the department that rations food and other necessities. **<u>Reality.</u>** Our government has many more than four departments now, but the things covered by these four are all now practiced by our government. The "spin doctors" working for whoever is in power twist the truth to try to convince the people that whatever has happened is good for everyone, even if it is not. Like the Ministry of Love, our law enforcement occasionally gets out of hand at places like Ruby Ridge and Waco. The Department of Defense is our Ministry of Peace, but this is the one that I have few problems with. Our government now, like the Ministry of Plenty, distributes and even rations food and other necessities to many. It has attempted to take over and ration health care.

The story has the countries citizens divided into two groups. The upper class are those who work for the government and have the most benefits. The lower class is everyone else just trying to make ends meet the best they can. **Reality.** The number of government workers has been growing rapidly. In general, government workers make more money, have better benefits, and work less. Everyone outside government works at least in part to support the government.

In the book you can be punished for how you think if it is considered a "thought crime". **Reality.** We now have hate crimes where a person can be punished more harshly for a crime they commit if it can be shown it was committed based on an unaccepted way of thinking. You can be fired from your job or required to attend sensitivity training to keep your job if it is determined your thinking is not politically correct and you used hate speech.

Children in the book were encouraged to turn in their parents if they think they are committing a crime. **Reality.** This is supposedly now true in some communist countries. In this country, children are encouraged to hide things they are taught at school from their parents. They are also encouraged to "educate" their parents about subjects the schools believe the parents are wrong about.

In the book the government is changing the meanings of words and encouraging "new speak". **<u>Reality.</u>** With politically correct speech we now have words that have been changed to mean what someone wants others to believe. Gay now means a homosexual when it used to mean happy. Progressive is used as a label for someone who is ultraliberal. The homeless are what used to be known as bums. Undocumented workers are what used to be called illegal aliens. Etc. etc. etc.

Love between a man and woman in the book was not allowed. Sexual relations and marriage were only allowed to produce children. **<u>Reality.</u>** Our society is moving quickly away from the traditional ideas of love and marriage. The word love is often used as a term to mean sex only. Marriages are not taken seriously, and many end in divorce. The entire idea of what marriage means is under attack and turned on its head.

The Ministry of Truth in the book is continuously working to change history. They recreate the past to say what the government wants it to be. **<u>Reality.</u>** Our schools and school books teach history according to what they want the children to know or not know. They often distort the truth by embellishing or deleting facts. The same historical "facts" are taught differently in different countries based on what the governments want people to believe.

In the book the government teaches everyone that the evils of capitalism are what caused all the problems in the past. The government saved the people from the evil capitalists. **Reality.** The concept that capitalism is the best economic model has been under attack for a long time. Until recently, our government was continually putting restraints and regulations on business to control capitalism. We are often told by some that "big business" is the cause of most of our problems and only the government can protect you by controlling them.

In the book most people follow the government line without question. Those who defy the government are punished. **Reality.** Many people today believe what they are told by the politicians, the media, and the liberals without question or reason. When someone stands up and questions the actions of our government or liberal politicians they are ridiculed and demonized. One of the basic concepts of the book is that you repeat a lie until it becomes truth.

So, was George Orwell really wrong in his predictions? Look at how the Socialists have taken over the Democrat party.

Hummingbirds

I know that I have already done a piece on evolution but this one was too good to pass up.

I enjoy watching nature programs on TV and recently watched one on BBC about hummingbirds narrated by David Attenborough. Here is how he told it. Hummingbirds originally came from high in the Andes mountains of South America. It seems the flowers there had a problem. The mornings were so cool that the insects would not pollinate the flowers until the afternoon. The flowers did not like this so somehow, they did not explain how, the flowers had the hummingbirds created. Excuse the "created" word - I did not know how else to say it. But the flowers were still not happy. The insects still wanted to go for the nectar in the flowers in the afternoon and the flowers no longer wanted to be pollinated by insects. So, the flowers evolved into a deep narrow trumpetlike shape that the insects could not get into.

David Attenborough was just the narrator, so you could not see him, but I'll bet he had trouble keeping a straight face telling this.

<u>War</u>

The Constitution makes the President the commander in chief over the armed forces of the United States. It also gives Congress the exclusive right to declare war. Although I cannot find documentation to back this up, I believe this was meant to be another form of separation of powers.

Harry Truman was the first to commit US troops to fighting and dying without a declaration of war. He sent our servicemen to Korea as part of a UN "police action". Around one-half million American soldiers died in Korea without the American people having the chance to have their representatives vote on it.

Since that time numerous wars have been fought by the brave US servicemen without any declaration of war. The worst of these was the Viet Nam war. President Johnson started the war in Viet Nam in earnest for purely selfish reasons. Almost 60,000 Americans died there. Johnson refused to allow the military to fight the war in a way that they could win, then when asked why he did not just pull out, he said he did not want to go down in history as the first President to lose a war.

Recently, congress passed a "War Powers Act" basically giving up their right to declare war and turning over that right to the presidency. Congress needs to take back their Constitutional duty to be the ONLY ones to declare war. A president should have the ability to send troops into a situation where an emergency does not allow time to consult Congress. But, if there is a likelihood that our soldiers are in danger, he should be required to either get a declaration of war from Congress within 3 days or pull the troops out.

Once war is declared, Congress should lay out the reasons and goals, then get out of the way and let the military win the war. If there is a good enough reason to declare war, there is a good enough reason to win it. I am tired of seeing images on TV of soldiers badly maimed from fighting an undeclared war with no real definition of why we are fighting.

Climate Change

The current climate change debate used to be called global warming. That name fell out of favor when it could be shown that the world was not warming at a significant rate. But are the climate change alarmist correct? Yes, the climate is changing. But the question is why, and should we be alarmed?

Back in 1975, the alarmist told us we were heading into a new Ice Age and it could not be stopped. They now tell us that while they were mistaken then, they now know more about climate science, and cannot be mistaken this time. The history of the world is full of instances of scientists being wrong about one thing or another. I am not saying we should ignore what they are now saying. I just think we need to take a deep breath and look at the facts.

Up until about the 1400's the world was in a period of unusual warmth. That was followed by a period known as "the little ice age". While it was not an actual ice age, it was period of significantly colder weather. A good example of what it was like is the painting of Washington crossing the Delaware. In the painting there are ice chunks in the river. As anyone who lives in the area can tell you, the Delaware River does not have ice chunks that size in it in the winter. But the painting is accurate. They did back then. The little ice age ended around 1850, but it did not end abruptly. We were still coming out of it when I was young. I remember it being much cooler back in the 50's and 60's. So, when you see statistics about how much the weather has warmed in the past 100 years or so, just keep this in mind.

Are the current weather patterns something to be alarmed about, or is it just a normal shift? If it is not normal, then what is causing it and can we do anything about it?

Between 1900 and 2000, the increase in the world's population was three times greater than during the entire previous history of humanity. It totaled an increase from 1.5 to 6.1 billion in just 100 years. Not only do humans exhale CO_2, they all use the products produced by the industry the alarmists blame for climate change. So, is the population growth mostly to blame for any rise in greenhouse gases?

I recently heard that scientists have found that the polar axis of the Earth is shifting at an alarming rate caused by some conditions in

China and India, and that is contributing to the climate changing.

You can argue about volcanos and other emitters of CO2. The animal rights people even want to blame it on cows. My main problem is how much can you trust people who are being paid to promote the idea. Not only are many college professors receiving government grants, but people like Al Gore are getting rich!

Reparations

In the 1600's King James II and Oliver Cromwell sold thousands of Irish into slavery in the Caribbean and Virginia. The liberal fact checkers try to deny this by calling them "indentured servants". The slave owners loved it because they spoke English, and they sold for much less than African slaves. They were also treated much worse than African slaves because they were the hated Catholics. As an American of Irish descent, I DEMAND reparations for myself and ALL Americans of Irish descent!

Now, let us talk about the Chinese......

<u>ESL</u>

Our Schools now teach "English as a Second Language" – ESL. They teach this to any student who is in school that does not speak English. They also teach these children their lessons in the language they speak, until they learn English. For some reason, this may take many years. Could it be because they receive government money?

I once worked with a man of Mexican heritage that was a third generation American. His wife was a second generation American. But they only spoke Spanish at home, and as a result, his children had to go through ESL at the cost of my tax dollar. People like this should have to pay the cost to teach their children English.

I was raised in a fair-sized city on the border with Mexico. Back then, whenever a student started school that only spoke Spanish, there was little extra effort to help. They had to learn to speak English quickly. And guess what? They did!

What we need to teach is English as a FIRST language!

<u>Mexico Will Pay For It</u>

Donald Trump campaigned on building a "big beautiful wall" and having Mexico pay for it. He is still working on the wall, but you do not hear him talk of Mexico paying for it any longer. But there is an easy way to do it.

I grew up in El Paso, Texas. When I was young there was a pedestrian only bridge to walk over the border to Juarez, Mexico. You had to pay a 2-cent fee on the American side, and a 1-cent fee on the Mexican side. Supposedly it was to pay the cost of building the bridge, but the bridge had long been paid for. This was a FEE, not a TAX.

I propose we do the same on every border crossing, but much higher. Charge $1 for every person at every border crossing plus $5 for each automobile. Charge for trucks and trains that cross. Charge $25 for every person that flies in or out of Mexico. Then use the money to fund our immigration system including building the wall.

(I have sent this idea to the President, my 2 senators, and several in the media I thought had connections - with no response.)

Impeachment

The word impeachment is the same as inditement. It is just bringing charges against someone. It is not finding the person guilty, or removing them from office. That only happens in the second half of the process where the individual is put on trial before the Senate and found guilty. It can be used for other than removing a president. Federal judges are removed on a fairly frequent basis through impeachment, and recently there was even talk about impeaching a member of the DOJ.

The Constitution of the United States says a president can be removed through the impeachment process for "treason, bribery and high crimes and misdemeanors", whatever that means. President Andrew Johnson, who was Lincoln's vice president and became president upon Lincoln's death, was the first to be impeached. Congress was angry with him because he wanted to be lenient on the south during reconstruction. He was not, however, convicted and removed from office.

Richard Nixon was the next president to have impeachment charges brought against him. When I think of Nixon, the image that comes to mind is of him on TV telling the American people "I am not a crook." It was and is a real shame it ever came to that. Yes, he was a crook. But compared to the two previous presidents before him, he was an amateur. Nixon had three problems. The easy one to understand is the problem that he got caught. Next, he tried to cover it up. Had he just admitted the problem and got someone to be the fall guy, it would have all blown over. But the thing he could not control was the Democrats and the liberal media smelled blood. They were determined to bring Nixon down. Not because he was a bad president. If they felt that way they would have gone after Kennedy and Johnson. He was not even much of a conservative. His only real guilt was he was a Republican. Remember, since Hoover was replaced by saint FDR, any Republican president was bad. Then, to their shame, his own party turned against him and asked him to resign. Had they stuck by him the way the Democrats stuck by Clinton; he would have survived. By letting the Democrats and the press get away with this, a precedent was set that has caused troubles between the parties to this day.

Clinton was the next to be impeached. In spite of everyone in the press saying differently, I believe Clinton was much worse than Nixon and deserved to be impeached. However, I see where the Republicans also smelled blood, and unwisely decided they would get revenge for what the Democrats did to Nixon. Like Andrew Johnson, Clinton was not convicted. This time, because the Democrats stood together and would not vote to convict one of their own.

The problem now is that too many people think impeachment is the thing to do if you disagree with the outcome of an election, or disagree with a president's policies. Maxine Watters started yelling "impeach 45!" the day Donald Trump took office. This is insane! What is more insane is all the Democrats and liberal media that keep this talk going. I think, and this is just my opinion, that the Democrats were scared to death that Trump would succeed. If he did, it would prove that everything they have said and done for decades has been a lie. So, they must bring him down.

We need a constitutional amendment that spells out exactly how and why a president can be removed from office. This nonsense has to stop!

Since I originally wrote this, the Democrats have used the pandemic, and voter fraud to bring President Trump down. They even brought a second impeachment in an effort to keep him from ever running again.

Re-election

You probably think you send people to Congress to represent you. Wrong! Members of congress are there for one reason, and one reason only. That is to get reelected. Yes, they do some things for their constituents. But their only motivation is to get reelected. The reason is simple. Money, and power which brings more money. Also, keep in mind that many, if not most of them, represent their party, not those that voted them into office.

Refineries

I lived in the Houston area for close to 30 years and worked in and around the refineries on the Houston ship channel. Yes, they stink. But I never heard of anyone getting seriously sick from the smell or wanting to close these plants because of it. To the people living close to the refineries, it smells like money!

The Electoral College

You hear a lot of talk lately about abolishing the Electoral College. I have to wonder if these people really understand what it is and why it was established. Back when the Constitution was being established, the delegates realized that when it came to electing a president, the cities of Boston, New York, and Philadelphia would be the only ones that decided who got elected president because they had such large populations compared to some other entire states back then. The Electoral College was devised to stop that. Today you have the same thing in a different way. Without the Electoral College the states of California, New York, and Florida could carry the entire election. Liberals would love this, but it would not be fair to the rest of the country.

Look at any map of who won the vote by county. I will clearly show that President Trump carried the vast number of counties in this country in 2016 and several entire states. Should not their votes count too?

Political Prosecution

There was a district attorney in Travis County (Austin), Texas named Ronnie Earle. He was famous for bringing trumped up charges on people he disagreed with politically. He got away with it for many years because Austin is a very liberal area, and he only attacked conservatives. Then he took on a Texas congressman named Tom Delay. While he was fairly successful at ruining Tom Delay's career, he also brought a bright light on himself. While the press and Democrats defended him by pointing out that he had prosecuted many Democrats in his career, they avoided saying that when he had done that, Texas was a solid Democratic state, and he only prosecuted Democrats that were conservative. His reign faded after the Delay case.

There have been many recent instances of political prosecution. There was the Duke Lacrosse case, and more recently the Baltimore police officers. In both of these cases the prosecutors knew the defendants were not guilty but prosecuted anyway because of political reasons.

I believe political prosecution should be against the law. It should be a felony with stiff penalties. However there needs to be a clear definition of what it is so prosecutors cannot be threatened just for doing their jobs.

<u>Scandinavian Countries</u>

The Socialist Democrats point to Scandinavian countries as examples of socialism succeeding. Three points to remember. First, they all benefit from North Sea oil which they use to pay for these programs. Second, they never went completely socialist. Third, they are all slowly moving away from socialism because they have found that even though they can pay for it, socialism does not work.

China

After World War II, the followers of Mao Tse-tung took control of all of China except the island of Formosa (now called Taiwan), and formed a communist government. At the time, the US recognized the Chinese government in Taiwan as the only legitimate government of all of China. In 1972, President Nixon visited communist China, and established formal relations with the communist government. For some time after that the US recognized both Chinese governments, but has since then dropped recognition of the government in Taiwan.

I think this was a mistake. I want to blame Nixon, but to be fair, it would have eventually happened anyway. The reason it was inevitable is the liberal mindset that it is foolish to ignore the reality that the communists are in fact in control of the country. They use the same argument with Cuba. However, there is a difference between recognizing facts, and giving diplomatic recognition. By giving China diplomatic recognition, it opens the door for open trade and travel. By not giving this recognition, it isolates a country and pressures them to change.

As trade with China increased, they became more powerful because the government virtually controls all business there. At least part of every dollar spent on Chinese goods goes to the government. And they spend a good part of that on building their military. We stayed significantly ahead of China in military technology until the Clinton presidency. Bill Clinton made it much easier for the Chinese to acquire US technology. He also helped China join the World Trade Organization. I cannot prove it, but it appears to be payback for Chinese financial support for his elections. (Which is illegal.)

I do not know the exact details, but Congress passed a law some time back giving preferential trade status called "Most Favored Nation" to some countries. In order to receive this status, any totalitarian country must have the President of the United States certify once a year that the country had improved the way it treats its citizens in the past year. For diplomatic reasons, we gave China this status, and the President dutifully certified it each year. This stopped with the admission of China into the WTO.

Some years back, the sign on the outside of all Wal Mart stores had a statement about selling only products made in the USA. Now, almost everything in those stores and every other store in America is made in China. The Chinese are awash in dollars coming from America. They use part of that money to buy properties in America and US bonds, and a great deal of it to improve their military capabilities. We not only gave them our jobs and our money, but we now are deeply in debt to them. We have given them the power to bully us not only financially, but militarily. The Chinese military have almost caught up with ours. Their military leaders openly challenge us and appear to believe they can win any war with us.
.

Our government needs to stop giving China preferential treatment. But more than that, the American people need to stop buying Chinese goods. We need to stop buying Chinese products and stop buying stock in companies that move jobs to China. When the Chinese devalue their currency to give them trade advantages, we need to raise tariffs to counter it.

Now that China has unleashed Covid on the world, the US needs to seize all Chinese assets in the US and disavow our debt to them and give the money to Americans who lost love ones, businesses, or took any kind of loss due to the Chinese virus.

A famous quote from Joseph Stalin said something like "we will hang the Americans and they will sell us the rope to do it." Stalin was wrong with the USSR, but he may have been right with China.

Smoking

I will bet most of you are not aware that in the 1950's children "smoked" candy cigarettes. They were a white candy stick with a red tip to look like it was lit. Nobody questioned it at the time since most adults smoked. In fact, almost everyone portrayed in the movies smoked. I am not sure why, but my parents did not smoke. I smoked my first cigarette when I was about 12, and by 16 I was smoking regularly. I smoked 2 packs a day for over 25 years before I quit. I just decided one day that it was bad for my health, and quit cold turkey.

As a reformed smoker I now see how foolish it was to smoke, and how offensive it can be to others. So, I did not object to the movement to stop people from smoking in public places. Now, however, I see these same people that objected so strenuously to cigarettes are pushing the legalization of marijuana. As I understand the reports I have read, marijuana is just as bad on your lungs as cigarettes. It is more addictive than nicotine, and I heard about one study that showed smoking marijuana kills brain cells that do not regenerate.

The argument you often hear is about its medical uses. However, the ingredient in marijuana that has medical properties can be put in a pill. The truth is they all just want to get high.

Political Courts

The United States is a unique country. It is 50 simi-sovereign states existing together as one sovereign country. This would appear to be an almost impossible arrangement. The founding fathers put the following in the Constitution to make it clear how it would work. "The powers not delegated to the United States by the Constitution, nor prohibited by it to the States, are reserved to the States respectively, or to the people." This amendment is the one thing that prevents a political party or a president from becoming a dictator. The glue that holds it all together is the Supreme Court. That is why it is essential that the court is kept non-political. A political court like the socialist Democrats have used to get their way for more than 50 years will inevitably lead to a dictatorship.

The First Amendment

The first 10 amendments to the constitution are referred to as the bill of rights. They were enacted because the original colonies would not sign the proposed constitution unless they were provided some guarantees of the rights of citizens and the states being formed. They were specifically intended to define and limit the power of the federal government. I am only going to address the first amendment here.

Congress shall make no law respecting an establishment of religion or prohibiting the free exercise thereof; or abridging the freedom of speech, or of the press; or the right of the people peaceably to assemble, and to petition the Government for a redress of grievances.

You will notice it covers 4 different "rights". Many people consider these rights to be absolute. But, in fact, they are not. A religion cannot include bigamy as a right. A famous quote from a previous Supreme Court justice said the freedom of speech does not cover the right to yell fire in a crowded theater. The freedom of the press is limited with libel laws. And in most places, you must get a permit to assemble in large groups. There is an old saying that your right to make a fist ends where my nose begins. Over the years the courts have ruled there are many limitations to these so-called rights. In the following I will address each of the four parts.

Freedom of Religion

To understand the "Freedom of Religion" issue, you must understand the history behind it. I realize many in this country never learned American history because of our failed education system. So, for those who do not know, I will briefly go over why this was so important to those who founded our country.

The first Americans were mostly ancestors of people who came from England, and were, up until that time, subjects of the king of England. England, like every other European country, was at one time part of the Church of Rome under the leadership of the Pope. The king of England had a dispute with Rome in 1534 and declared that all England would from that time forward no longer be part of the Church of Rome nor answer to the Pope. The only thing that really changed was that from that point forward, the king, not the Pope was the head of the church in England. The Church of England was supported by the government, and all expenses came out of the country's treasury. Citizens may believe in other forms of worship, but they had no choice in paying taxes to support the Church of England. Those who did not attend the Church of England were often discriminated against.

Because many of the colonies were originally formed by subjects of the crown that wanted to get away from what they felt was the tyranny of the state-run church, there were some very strong feelings on this subject. Notice that there are two parts to the sentence. Congress shall pass no law with regards to the establishment of a religion. And Congress shall pass no law denying free exercise of religious beliefs. This was done to be sure nothing like what had happened in England would ever happen in the new country of The United States of America.

The terms "Freedom of Religion" and "Separation of Church and State" do not appear anywhere in the Constitution. What is there is often referred to as the "Establishment Clause." There are writings by some of the founding fathers that expand on what was intended, including a statement by Thomas Jefferson about building a wall of separation between church and state. The courts have proven to take a very liberal attitude on what is meant by this amendment. While I read this as *Congress* shall make no law, the courts read it as no form of government can get involved in religion in any way. While I read it as prohibiting the free exercise thereof, the courts have interpreted it as unless it offends somebody. I believe the courts have, in fact, ruled against the intent and the letter of what is written in the amendment. It appears they have felt the need to expand it to cover whatever any person or group have complained about. I see no problem having a Christmas display on a city government's property if that is what the majority of the citizens in that jurisdiction want. Congress passed no law requiring it. It is especially none of the courts business if it is paid for by private funds. Are the courts interfering with the citizens right to the free exercise of religion? If we must remove everything from government property that offends anyone for any reason, I must say I am offended by some of the judges that are there. So, should they be removed?

For a person, a group, or even a government to express religious beliefs is not establishing a state-run religion. Nobody is being forced to participate. I agree there is a fine line with the issue of tax monies being spent. But if you cannot spend tax monies unless everyone agrees on what it is being spent for, none will ever be spent. (Although thinking about that, it might not be a bad idea!) Seriously though, in a democratic republic like we have, the majority rules. As long as the individual is not irreparably harmed, they need to just suck it up and accept it.

What about my right to the free exercise of my beliefs? Have the courts gone too far and denied me my rights? While I agree there are times, like the bigamy issue stated above, that the government has a right to intervene, I believe the courts are the ones that have in fact made themselves the dictators of religion in this country. They have told me I cannot celebrate Christmas unless I also celebrate Passover, Ramadan and atheism. They have told me I cannot have my children taught my moral and religious beliefs but must have them taught evolution and sex education. They have even told me that if my belief that murder is a moral sin does not count if my 16-year-old daughter wants an abortion.

I am a strong believer in keeping government out of religion. I think once you give government a little power in any area, they will eventually take it all. But we need to remember the courts are part of our government. The first amendment was supposed to protect our right to our religious beliefs. But in this country, this right, just like any right, is only as good as the courts rule.

Freedom of the Press

The right of the freedom of the press is written in the amendment like an afterthought to the freedom of speech. If you think about it, they are both basically the same thing. If you have the right to speak something, then you should be able to write it down and publish it. While I strongly agree with this basic principle, there are several problems that need to be addressed.

The press is not just about reporting news. From the beginning it has been used for political purposes through editorials and political satire. Everyone should be aware of this and accept it. The problem is when the line between what is legitimate news and being political is blurred. For some time now, newspapers and broadcast news have reported the news with a political slant. They decide which candidate or issue they support, and report or fail to report the news in a way that favors their side. This has gone on for years to the great advantage of some politicians. Until recently, this has mostly been done for liberal politicians or issues without the press being held accountable. Lately though, with the advent of the internet and conservative news outlets, all of a sudden some are crying foul! It was OK to slant the news, and even sometimes make up the news for a liberal or Democrat, but when someone favors a conservative politician or issue, that is wrong and must be stopped. The liberals have lost their monopoly, and they don't like it. It is amazing how nasty some of this has become.

"The press" believe that their right is absolute. While they decry what some people say, and write editorials about how these people should be silenced, they will fight to the bitter end to publish anything they want to. The New York Times fights for their right to publish classified government documents that are leaked to them. They seem to think the public's right to know is more important than the security of our country. But let them get a document leaked to them that makes a liberal politician look bad, and they will cover it up. They think the public has no right to know that. It seems that the freedom of the press includes the right not to report anything that may harm their causes. Maybe it is not fair to single out the NYT since many others do the same. I just could not help digging them since they are one of the worst. Besides, I have the right under the freedom of the press to publish my opinions in my essays. But I try to be as factual as possible. I state as often as I think necessary that these are my opinions.

There has been an accusation lately that the press is the "enemy of the people". Is the press our enemy? NO! A free press is essential to a free democracy. However, when "news" corporations and individuals who call themselves the press use that position to lie to the people in order to sway political beliefs, they are the enemy of the people. But how do you know who is lying? By listening to every point of view then using the good sense God gave you

I don't believe in limiting the press in any way other than libel and legitimate state secrets. The freedom of the press is an important part of keeping all our other freedoms. I would just like them to be a little more honest about it. Report ALL the news without bias. Be as complete and factual as possible. Don't make up or repeat lies. If you are not sure something is factual, investigate it. That is your job! Keep your opinions on the editorial pages. The press has an almost sacred duty to the people of this country, and they are failing in that duty. Miserably!

The Freedom of Assembly

There is really not much controversy on this subject. But there are some things worth looking at.

First, look at the word "peaceably". In other words, you do not have the right to riot in the streets no matter how much you think you are petitioning the government for a redress of your grievances. When people use an event or other problem as an excuse to riot, steal, and destroy, they should be held accountable by law. I'm tired of the law looking the other way because someone thinks these people have a right to be upset.

Everyone also needs to understand and accept that this right applies to everyone. It applies to the KKK just as much as the NAACP. It applies to Christian groups and Muslim groups and atheist alike. It applies to liberal groups and conservative groups. If you don't agree with a group, the best way to combat anyone or group that you think extreme is to ignore them. When you counter protest, you just get them on TV. But if they have enough followers, maybe someone needs to look at their grievances. While they may be extreme or wrong on many of their views, if they have a large following, there is probably a legitimate basis for at least some of their complaint. If you listen to and solve the legitimate complaints of any group, the extremists will be all that is left and will eventually fade away.

The Tea Party has just as much right to assemble as the Climate Change movement. It does not matter if you agree with their position or not. Do not try to stop someone from gathering and speaking, unless you are willing to let someone do the same to you.

The Freedom of Speech

I deliberately left this one until last even though it should have been before the freedom of the press. Be forewarned. I am going to freely exercise my freedom of speech in some of the things I am about to say.

I do not know who said it, but there is a famous quote that goes something like this. I may not agree with what you have to say, but I will defend to the death your right to say it. Benjamin Franklin said "whoever would overthrow the liberty of a nation, must begin by subduing the freeness of speech".

We have already lost the right to free speech in this country. Or maybe it would be more accurate to say that we willingly gave it away. The only freedom we now have is the freedom to say anything that will not offend some person or group. The only exception being if we want to use profanities. That is OK even if it offends someone. I said this previously, but it is worth repeating. The very fact that there is an accepted term in this country "politically correct speech" should scare the hell out of all Americans. I disagree with the KKK and the NAACP. I disagree with the ACLU and the white supremacists. But those are my opinions. Just because I disagree with any person or group does not mean I have a right to silence them. When any group or government succeeds in silencing the people that they disagree with or that disagrees with them, dictatorial rule will soon follow.

What kind of limitations should apply? It is very strange that the same people that try to limit your speech as offensive to some people, believe they have the right to use whatever foul, vulgar language they want in public. I once was at a parade standing on a curb of a public street with my wife and then very young daughter. Two boys in their teens were standing next to us and every other word that came out of their mouths were profanities. When I asked them to stop, one of them told me he had the right to speak in whatever manner he wanted. I answered I would get a cop and let him explain that right to him. The boys moved to another location to offend other people. While it is true that using profanity in public was once against the law everywhere and still is in most places, people are rarely charged with it anymore. Judges usually dismiss the charges citing their right to free speech. I don't care what the liberal judges think. There are some words that are so patently offensive to most people they should not be allowed in public. That includes much of the current RAP music.

Then there are those people who think that by mispronouncing a profanity makes it OK. I am getting tired of hearing freaking this or frigging that. Everyone knows what you mean, and since your made-up word means the same as the offensive word, it is just as offensive. If you want to argue the point, let me ask you if your spouse is freaking anyone else. Does that offend you?

The same people who want to have the freedom to use profanities are the biggest defenders of politically correct speech. To be politically correct, you cannot say a person is a queer any more. You should call them gay. Nonsense! The word gay means happy, and there is no reason to believe they are happier than anyone else. There is ample evidence they are different from the vast majority, which would make them queer. People with disabilities are not disabled anymore. They are challenged. Nonsense! Everyone has challenges, but their abilities have been limited. So, they are disabled. Some say you can't even call a terrorist a terrorist anymore. You might offend them! But the ultimate worst example of politically correct speech is you must say "the N word" rather than saying - dare I say it? Nigger.

Let us look at the word nigger, and what it really means. It is just a mispronunciation of the word Negro. But, you say, it was used as a derogatory term by white people in the past. Not true. While there were many in the past, and sadly some who still do think black people are inferior, any way they would have referred to those same people would be thought of as derogatory. If they used to call them black in the past, would we now have to say "the B word"? There is a very good reason why black people are offended by the word nigger. It is because they themselves have made it into a derogatory term. They use it as an insult when referring to other blacks. It is usually ones they feel have sold out to the whites, but they can use it as a general insult. But they only use it against other blacks. So, they themselves have made it into a derogatory term pertaining only to blacks. So, when they hear a white person use the word nigger, they feel it is an insult to all blacks. On the other hand, black people feel free to use words like "whitey," "honky," and "cracker," to refer to white people. And those terms are definitely meant as insulting.

Now we also have "hate speech". This also poses a problem. What is hate speech? Who determines what it is? I watch protests on TV where they are carrying signs decrying hate. Then they speak of hating everything they disagree with. Many even say they hate America!

The courts have ruled there is a freedom of expression that is included in the freedom of speech. But again, it depends on who it offends. You can hang fake bull's balls from your pickup, but you better not display a swastika. You can put the American flag in a toilet and call it art, but you cannot fly the Confederate flag. You can display a crucifix in a bottle of urine, but you should never erect a cross in a park. I agree expression is a part of speech. But it should apply evenly and with some common sense.

Let me repeat my opening statement. I may not agree with what you have to say, but I will defend to the death your right to say it. We just need to add that we should temper it with a large dose of civility, and not limit it with being politically correct.

<u>Guns Crossing State Lines</u>

Senator Dick Durbin of Illinois stated recently that one of the reasons for the gun violence in his state is the easy accessibility of guns in his neighboring state if Indiana. That begs the question – why does not Indiana have the same problems.

Vacation

My family traveled on vacation a lot when I was young, and I still do to this day. I have been blessed to see many of the National Parks and other wonders in this great country. Now, however, it is hard to get in some places, and if you get in you are forced to ride tour busses to reduce the traffic. It wouldn't be so bad if it was just Americans enjoying our parks, but what you find is that the majority are foreigners. I am not advocating being prejudiced against foreigners. It is just that what is ours is ours. I think we should limit the number of foreign visitors allowed in places like the Grand Canyon so that Americans can enjoy them.

Motorcycles

Why are motorcycles allowed to have such loud mufflers? If my car was that loud, I would get a ticket. Also, have you ever noticed there are 2 kinds of motorcycle drivers? The Harley type that ride big hogs in large groups and drive so slow as to make sure everyone notices them. Then there is the Kawasaki type that drives suicidal in freeway traffic or over mountain passes.

Government Subsidies

For any government, ours or foreign, to subsidize any product or industry is an attempt to manipulate commerce in a way that is against capitalistic principles. The politicians give a lot of high-sounding arguments for doing it, but it is always counterproductive in the long run.

Our government subsidizes dairy products by buying a large portion of their production. They do this to reduce the supply which will drive up the price because of demand. The government uses what they can for the military etc., then gives the rest away in welfare. As a result, the consumer pays very high prices for items like cheese products, while others get it for free.

Many of our subsidies are in the agricultural area. We pay farmers NOT to grow certain crops so as to keep up the prices. We even buy up and destroy crops that have been overproduced. The result of this is it encourages farmers to overproduce or announce their intention to plant a crop they know the government will pay them not to plant.

There are also now ethanol subsidies. The government wants to encourage farmers to grow corn to make ethanol as a fuel additive. As a result, too many acres are planted in corn which drives up the cost to the consumer of other produce.

Any help a government gives any business gives them an advantage. It can be in the form of direct subsidies, or tax breaks. But whenever it happens, someone else has to pay the price for it. It is often used to give a business an advantage in sales to other countries. But all this does is make the other countries do whatever is needed to counter the advantage.

Our government should severally limit any subsidies it gives. If a foreign government subsidizes a product to give them an unfair advantage in trade, we should tax that product enough to at least take that advantage away

Work Ethic

There is very little work ethic left in this country. While it is true, youth have always had to learn to function in business, the young people today think the employer owes them a job and there is no good reason to expect them to work for their pay. I said young people, but this is unfortunately true of people in their 30's and 40's also. And whatever made people think it is acceptable to stab coworkers in the back to get ahead? Is that something taught in college these days?

American Indians

I have traveled all over the US, and lived in many places in the southwest. I have had the privilege of meeting and knowing some American Indians. I have never met one that I did not only like, but find to be an exceptionally nice person. However, I do have some bones to pick with them.

American Indians take exception to being referred to as savages in the movies and history books. However, they were savages. But, because the white men in those times were also savages, and better at it, the Indians did not have a chance. If the Indians had learned their lesson from Sitting Bull at Little Big Horn and banded together, they might have won. But the Indians were too busy killing each other to make any effort to combine their forces. In fact, it has been said that there are more Indians alive today than would have been if we had not forced them on reservations. We stopped them from killing each other. The Navaho and Hopi still fight to this day because they cannot get along and live so close to each other.

You often hear of the injustices by the white man in massacres like the one at Wounded Knee. But the Indians were just as guilty of committing atrocities. We need to put the past behind us by admitting we both were guilty of some wrongs, and move on.

I don't care what some idiot judge has ruled, the Indian tribes are not sovereign. They cannot be sovereign and still be American citizens. You can argue that we made treaties with them, and you don't make treaties with your own citizens. However, they were not citizens then. If the current Indians alive here in the US today want to claim sovereignty, they should stop claiming US citizenship and taking any US government money as a first step. I doubt that it will ever get to a second step.

What is needed, is for every American to be an American first. All Americans born in the US are native Americans. We need to stop distinguishing American Indians as different from other Americans. Do away with the reservations and just give the land to them divided equally or buy it from them. Then give them whatever assistance is needed to have them integrate into society. But put a time limit on it.

They have already been wards of the state for too long.

I know most Indians and many others will take great exception to my opinions on this. But we are really doing them a great injustice by allowing the status quo.

<u>**Banning Books**</u>

Every totalitarian government in the past century began with similar moves for change. One of those changes has always been banning, then burning books the government did not approve of. Soviet Russia, Nazi Germany, Communist China, Cuba, Venezuela, all did it. We have been eliminating some books like Huckleberry Finn because it supposedly "offends" some people. Now, I hear that some school libraries are eliminating more, including one of the greatest literary works of the 20th century, "To Kill A Mockingbird." I cannot believe so many Americans are willing to turn their country over to the Socialist Democrat censors. As always happens when totalitarianism takes over, it is extremely hard to take your freedoms back.

__Illegal Aliens__

The problem of people entering this country illegally, or staying after visas expire, is monumental. It is too much for me to adequately address here, but I am going to try to tackle just some issues concerning those coming in from Mexico. I know the liberals want to call them "undocumented workers" or "undocumented migrants", but if they are undocumented, that means they are here illegally. If they are from another country, they are an alien. So, I choose not to be politically correct, but to call them what they are. Illegal Aliens.

The first thing you need to understand is that the government of Mexico encourages their citizens to go north to the US to work. They don't care if it is legal or not. They even provide as much assistance as possible on their side of the border and try to use our courts against us on this side. The reason for this is simple. One of the largest sources of money in the economy of Mexico comes from dollars being sent home by Mexicans working in the US. If that was to stop, the economy of Mexico would collapse. Because Mexico is on our border, if that was to happen it would cause big problems in this country.

There used to be a "bracero program" in this country. It was a method of allowing cheap labor into the country to harvest crops, mostly in California. Under the program, our government could keep track of who was here. But the unions did not like it. They wanted higher paid union labor working the fields. When JFK was president, the unions talked him into doing away with the program. Unfortunately, that did not stop the farms from getting their low paid workers from Mexico. The only thing that changed was they were now here illegally, and the government had no control.

Because our citizens are spoiled and insist on high wages and low prices, businesses have to find a way to give the consumer what they demand. Many simply went overseas for their production where the cost of labor is much lower. However, some things like housing cannot be produced overseas. So, over time, cheap labor from Mexico has been used for much more than just harvesting produce. The unions now have given up trying to stop it and have reversed their stand to where they now want to unionize them.

The problem with the Mexican economy is rarely addressed. But the reason it is not addressed is that the politicians have other reasons for not wanting to do anything about illegal aliens. Both parties take contributions from businesses that use illegal labor. The politicians defend these businesses by claiming the illegals are only hired to do work Americans won't do. This has made them make such silly statements as the one John McCain once said. He said he would pay $20 an hour (I don't remember the exact amount) to any man willing to pick lettuce in the hot fields in Yuma. The next day his Phoenix office had a line around the block of people wanting to take him up on the offer. No, Americans for the most part will not pick lettuce in the hot Yuma sun for what the growers pay. And Americans would not buy lettuce if the price went up because the growers had to pay higher wages. So, I can see the problem with produce farms.

However, it is not just produce anymore. Much of the poultry and meat cutting industry jobs have been taken over by illegal labor. Many good, high paying construction jobs including almost all of the homebuilding jobs are taken by illegals. Illegals have even taken much of the work in the fast-food restaurants that once were held by our youth as entry level jobs. In these cases, no one can legitimately argue that it is jobs no Americans will take. You often hear these jobs go to illegals because, unlike Americans, they are very hard workers. To a large degree, that is true. But what you seldom hear discussed is quality. The Mexican laborer has no concept craftsmanship. The homes build today are very low quality compared to when American labor built them. The construction industry uses illegal labor for the only reason that they can make a higher profit with the lower wages. You know from my previous essays that I am a capitalist. But that does not mean that there are not still some problems with it.

Another problem can be laid squarely at the feet of the Democratic party. But the Republicans would do the same if they could. The great majority of voters of Mexican heritage vote Democrat. The Democrats see every illegal as a possible new citizen that will then vote for them. So, every Democrat not only does not want to do anything about illegal aliens, they are anxious to give them legal status as the first step to citizenship.

The answer is to again establish a program like the old bracero program. Under the program, no one should be allowed to hire an employee from another country unless it can be shown no American wants the job. When an employer hires someone from a country like Mexico, they should be responsible for all costs to transport them to and from their location and should be responsible to report to the government if the worker disappears. The business hiring the foreign worker MUST provide adequate health insurance. No tax dollar should be spent providing medical service for the worker. The foreign worker should not be allowed to bring their family with them. I know that seems heartless, but if they need the work badly enough they will have to sacrifice. Then the foreign worker must return home for at least one month every year. Foreign workers may send all or part of their wages home if they wish, but no government benefits or checks should be sent to a foreign address. I am aware these changes will necessitate that prices for some goods in America will rise. But other costs like tax payer paid benefits will go down and this is an area that Americans must make part of the sacrifice.

Yes, there are challenges to overcome. But we can solve them if we can just get the politicians out of the way.

Photo Radar

I think photo radar is unconstitutional. The sixth amendment gives you the right to confront and question your accuser. But who is the accuser in these cases? A camera? A radar machine? How do you put them on the stand to cross examine? The prosecution can put an expert on the stand to swear the machine is designed to record your image and speed, but as with any machine, they could malfunction or not work as designed. You could carry this argument to any accusation based on radar. The officer on the roadside is just the one reading the machine. The machine is the one accusing you of speeding. In cases of a defendant being criminally accused, only a human accuser that can be questioned by the defendant should be allowed.

The Beaver Dam

This story has made the rounds on the internet for some time and is reported to be true. Whether it is true or not, it makes some good points. It begins with a letter from a government agency to a citizen, followed by his response.

State of Pennsylvania's letter to Mr. DeVries: SUBJECT: DEQ File No.97-59-0023; T11N; R10W, Sec 20; Lycoming County

Dear Mr. DeVries:
It has come to the attention of the Department of Environmental Quality that there has been recent unauthorized activity on the above referenced parcel of property. You have been certified as the legal landowner and/or contractor who did the following unauthorized activity:

Construction and maintenance of two wood debris dams across the outlet stream of Spring Pond.

A permit must be issued prior to the start of this type of activity. A review of the Department's files shows that no permits have been issued. Therefore the Department has determined that this activity is in violation of Part 301, Inland

Lakes and Streams, of the Natural Resource and Environmental Protection Act, Act 451 of the Public Acts of 1994, being sections 324.30101 to 324.30113 of the Pennsylvania Compiled Laws, annotated.

The Department has been informed that one or both of the dams partially failed during a recent rain event, causing debris and flooding at downstream locations. We find that dams of this nature are inherently hazardous and cannot be permitted. The Department therefore orders you to cease and desist all activities at this location, and to restore the stream to a free-flow condition by removing all wood and brush forming the dams from the stream channel. All restoration work shall be completed no later than January 31, 2007.

Please notify this office when the restoration has been completed so that a follow-up site inspection may be scheduled by our staff. Failure to comply with this request or any further unauthorized activity on the site may result in this case being referred for elevated enforcement action. We anticipate and would appreciate your full cooperation in this matter. Please feel free to contact me at this office if you have any questions.

Sincerely, David L. Price - District Representative and Water Management Division. Re: DEQ File No. 97-59-0023; T11N; R10W, Sec. 20; Lycoming County

Dear Mr. Price,

Your certified letter dated 12/17/06 has been handed to me to respond to. I am the legal landowner but not the Contractor at 2088 Dagget Lane, Trout Run, Pennsylvania.

A couple of beavers are in the (State unauthorized) process of constructing and maintaining two wood 'debris' dams across the outlet stream of my Spring Pond. While I did not pay for, authorize, nor supervise their dam project, I think they would be highly offended that you call their skillful use of nature's building materials 'debris.'

I would like to challenge your department to attempt to emulate their dam project any time and/or any place you choose. I believe I can safely state there is no way you could ever match their dam skills, their dam resourcefulness, their dam ingenuity, their dam persistence, their dam determination and/or their dam work ethic.

As to your request, I do not think the beavers are aware that they must first fill out a dam permit prior to the start of this type of dam activity.

My first dam question to you is: (1) Are you trying to discriminate against my Spring Pond Beavers, or (2) do you require all beavers throughout this State to conform to said dam request?

If you are not discriminating against these particular beavers, through the Freedom of Information Act, I request completed copies of all those other applicable beaver dam permits that have been issued.   (Perhaps we will see if there really is a dam violation of Part 301, Inland Lakes and Streams, of the Natural Resource and Environmental Protection Act, Act 451 of the Public Acts of 1994, being sections 324.30101 to 324.30113 of the Pennsylvania Compiled Laws, annotated.)

I have several dam concerns. My first dam concern is, aren't the beavers entitled to legal representation? The Spring Pond Beavers are financially destitute and are unable to pay for said representation -- so the State will have to provide them with a dam lawyer.

The Department's dam concern that either one or both of the dams failed during a recent rain event, causing flooding, is proof that this is a natural occurrence, which the Department is required to protect. In other words, we should leave the Spring Pond Beavers alone rather than harassing them and calling them dam names.

If you want the dammed stream 'restored' to a dam free-flow condition please contact the beavers -- but if you are going to arrest them, they obviously did not pay any attention to your dam letter, they being unable to read English.

In my humble opinion, the Spring Pond Beavers have a right to build their unauthorized dams as long as the sky is blue, the grass is green and water flows downstream. They have more dam rights than I do to live and enjoy Spring Pond. If the Department of Natural Resources and Environmental Protection lives up to its name, it should protect the natural resources (Beavers) and the environment (Beavers' Dams).

So, as far as the beavers and I are concerned, this dam case can be referred for more elevated enforcement action right now. Why wait until 1/31/2007? The Spring Pond Beavers may be under the dam ice by then and there will be no way for you or your dam staff to contact/harass them.

In conclusion, I would like to bring to your attention to a real environmental quality, health, problem in the area. It is the bears! Bears are actually defecating in our woods. I definitely believe you should be persecuting the defecating bears and leave the dam beavers alone. If you are going to investigate the beaver dam, watch your dam step! The bears are not careful where they dump!

Being unable to comply with your dam request, and being unable to contact you on your dam answering machine, I am sending this response to your dam office. THANK YOU, RYAN DEVRIES & THE DAM BEAVERS

Fashion

Fashion designers deliberately change fashions so that they can force the public to buy new products to stay up with what is in fashion. One of the easiest ways to show this is in men's ties. I have a closet full of ties, but I cannot wear any of them if I want to be "in style" Ties go from thin to wide, long to short, and change in what patterns are in style. Lately I have noticed that they are not narrowing the tie as it goes to the top as they always have, thereby making the knot look very big.

Recreational Drugs

I am probably going to step on a few toes here. I once believed the politicians did not want to do anything about the drug problem in this country because they were drug users too. I have now realized that a drug addicted population is one that is easier for them to control. Another reason they like drugs is that the taxes from legalized drugs are a guaranteed source of cash since the users are addicted. If you read this and think that "recreational" use of drugs is ok, I believe you are contributing to the problems we face in this great country.

JFK and the Assassination

I know there will be some who say that the following just proves I am a kook. But hear me out.

It is human nature to not want to believe one single person could be responsible for any great tragedy. As a result, when something like the JFK assassination happens, conspiracy theorists come out of the woodwork. While I usually do not put much stock in conspiracy theories, I have my own thoughts on this one. But to understand what I am about to say, you need a little background.

The election between Richard Nixon and John Kennedy was one of the closest in American History. The Kennedy campaign led by Joseph Kennedy, John's father, needed a little insurance to win. First, they named LBJ as vice president because he would be able to deliver enough fraudulent votes in Texas to win that state. They also managed to get the same in West Virginia. Then it came down to who would take the state of Illinois. Chicago mayor, Richard Daley Sr. stuffed the ballot boxes with enough fraudulent votes to sway Illinois to Kennedy. Everyone in politics and the news media knew Kennedy did not really win, but back then as now, it was accepted that the winner was the one who got away with the most dirty tricks. Nixon also accepted this and said nothing.

During the transition, Eisenhower told Kennedy of a plan he approved where the CIA was helping Cuban expatriates take back Cuba from Castro. Under the plan, if the expatriates experienced any trouble, the CIA and US troops would intervene in their behalf. When the day of the attack came and the expatriate forces were being beaten at the Bay of Pigs, Kennedy refused to send in the promised help. To this day many Americans of Cuban descent vote Republican as a result. The other result was more serious. The premier of the USSR, Nikita Khrushchev already believed he could beat the US in a war. Now he saw a serious weakness in the US leadership. He decided to establish a missile base in Cuba with nuclear warheads.

Kennedy did what any president would have to do in the situation. He called on the USSR to remove the missiles. To his credit, he resisted calls to send in US troops. However, he did negotiate behind the scenes to remove our missiles from Turkey as a trade-off while denying it to the US public. He lied to the

American people and was called a hero for doing it.

Kennedy was also a well-known womanizer. It was becoming an open secret but the press kept it under wraps as much as they could. But his affair with Marilyn Monroe was becoming too public and had the potential to become an embarrassment. Bobby Kennedy and the Kennedy's brother-in-law, actor Peter Lawford, visited Marylyn with two other men one night. The next morning Marilyn was found dead. Was she killed to protect Kennedy? Many believe so, but we may never know.

In spite of what you may have heard, Kennedy was not a very popular president. My parents, who were staunch Democrats, had a LP record that made fun of the Kennedy family. It was a very popular LP at the time. The reason Kennedy went to Texas was he was in so much hot water with his own party, he was going to a meeting to try to smooth things over. Just like FDR, the press and the Democrats want everyone to believe Kennedy was a saint. Had he not been assassinated; he would be remembered in history much differently.

The Assassination.
As I said before, Kennedy had many enemies; and many of them wanted him dead. One theory is Castro did it in retaliation for Kennedy trying to have him done away with. It is true Kennedy directed the CIA to try to kill Castro. Another theory is the mafia did it to stop Bobby Kennedy's investigations into their organizations. The theory being that to kill Bobby would just make JFK mad and make it worse on them. But to kill JFK would get Bobby removed from office. Then there is the famous theory of the New Orleans connection that the movie was made about. But there is a problem with all of these theories. They would all bring the full force of the American government and law enforcement down on them. No, the only way it could happen was if it was an inside job being orchestrated high enough to insure a complete cover up.

FBI director J. Edgar Hoover hated the Kennedys; all of them. He thought John was an embarrassment to the country. He did not like the family bootlegging history, and he really did not like the Kennedy brothers turning the White House into their sex orgy playground. But even he could not do it without help. Vice President Johnson also hated the Kennedys. John Kennedy picked him as Vice President only for political reasons. Kennedy thought Johnson was a Texas hick rube and treated him as such. Also, Johnson had been a very powerful person in Congress, but he left that to be VP so he would be next in line for the presidency. But now, Kennedy was openly saying he would not have Johnson on his re-election ticket. That would leave Johnson as a has been with no future.

If Hoover had the help of the man who would become president on Kennedy's death, he could get away with it. But Hoover also had the problem of getting someone to actually do it. He could not use anyone in the FBI, but some in the CIA also hated Kennedy because of his betrayal in the Bay of Pigs fiasco, and the CIA had just the kind of people hc needed. The CIA was also capable of setting up a patsy like Oswald.

There are a couple of problems concerning Oswald as the lone shooter that I cannot get over. First, it has been established he was not that good a marksman, especially with the old gun he had. He supposedly missed on the first shot – the one that was closest and he would have had time to take aim; but then supposedly hit Kennedy on 2 more shots in quick succession while operating the bolt action. Next, Oswald was seen by a police officer on the first floor of the book depository (and not out of breath) just minutes after the shots were fired. He would not have had the time to go down 6 floors.

I believe Oswald was a part of the conspiracy and may have fired the first shot. I believe there was at least one more shooter. Oswald was just an ignorant patsy put there to take the blame from the beginning. Hoover had the assassination plan executed through the CIA, and Johnson saw to it the truth was covered up. At first Johnson refused to have any investigation, but then assigned the Warren commission under pressure. But no one knows if the Warren commission did a good job or not because they sealed their findings.

If we had the time and space here, I could say more, but that is basically my theory.

Insurance

As I have said on several occasions, I am a capitalist. Insurance can be looked at as just another business working in the capitalist system. However, let me say up front that in general, I don't like insurance companies.

One reason I do not like them is the way they sell themselves and their product. To hear them talk, they are in business because they care about you and want to protect you from whatever disaster may happen from a dented fender to death. They are not your good neighbor. They do not want to put you in their good hands. And they are definitely not on your side. The truth is, they are in business to make a profit, and in a capitalist economy, that is the way it should be. But they lie to you to get your business, and then will look for any possible way not to pay when you have a claim. This has resulted in a sort of game being played where the consumer tries to find ways to overcome the insurance company's reluctance to pay.

Years ago, medical insurance would pay any claim without question. That encouraged doctors and hospitals to inflate their bills. Then, overnight, the insurance companies reversed course. They now tell the doctors and hospitals up front what they will pay, but still do little to check on if the charges are legitimate. This has resulted in another game being played between the medical profession and the insurance companies. But this game is rigged where only the consumer loses. The very fact insurance exists is the reason for the high price of medical service. On the one hand, doctors and hospitals could not get the prices they charge if it was not for insurance. On the other hand, the doctor's own insurance requires him to perform unnecessary tests to cover him in case of a lawsuit. I will admit that without insurance a doctor would be back to bartering his service for a chicken and some vegetables, and many of the important medical breakthroughs would never have happened.

Aside from medical insurance, I know from personal experience the insurance companies are responsible for running up prices elsewhere. Because they are willing to pay more than a repair or service is worth, prices soar. The insurance company does not take the loss. Your rates just go up. Again, from personal experience I know that body shops charge more than they should and home repairs are much higher priced than needed. Although it is easy to blame a crooked business for overcharging, what about an insurance agent that recommends them?

Insurance runs up the cost of almost everything. Every business must have insurance to protect them from accidents and lawsuits. And if their product is one that invites lawsuits, the insurance is very high, and the cost of their product goes up dramatically. A good example is ladder manufacturers. Every time some idiot falls off a ladder due to his own incompetence, the ladder manufacturer gets sued.

I saw a comedy once where an actor played the part of a man considering buying life insurance. He said that the insurance company was betting he would not die. It is true the insurance company is gambling. But they stack the odds in their favor. They are betting you will live long enough that the premiums you pay plus the interest they can make will add up to more than they have to pay out. They make you prove with a physical exam and checks on family medical history that there will not be much chance of you dying before then.

States are supposed to regulate insurance companies. In truth, the state governments are often their best allics. Insurance companies buy off politicians with campaign contributions. That is why insurance rates vary so much between states. The companies are more successful with their bribery in some states than others. You are also required to buy auto liability insurance in every state. On the surface, that makes a lot of sense. I do not want some irresponsible guy wrecking my car and I have to pay for it. But it may make more sense to be stricter on driving privileges and take the irresponsible people off the street. Or just make the irresponsible driver the one who has to buy the insurance.

Again, being a capitalist, I believe in the right of the insurance companies to be in business and make a profit. I would just like to see them be honest about what they are doing, and I would like to see a more honest relationship between them and my government.

Judicial Activism

Have you ever wondered why there is always a fight between Democrats and Republicans when it comes to the appointment of judges? Liberals realized long ago that most of their extreme ideas could never be passed as laws through Congress because the public would not stand for it. But, as judges began to take on the power of declaring law, the left realized if they could appoint sympathetic judges, they could have their way. During the 60's and 70's, when liberal thought had more acceptance than now, they were able to stack the courts with judges that would mandate laws.

The Constitution of the United States gives the legislative branch the sole authority to pass laws. If a judge believes a law needs to exist for any reason, let him run for Congress. A judge has no right to arbitrarily decide he thinks something is not fair, and then to force his views on the citizens.

Today, when liberal groups find something they do not like or want changed, they go shopping for a sympathetic judge and file suit in their district. Even if the judge is overturned, the liberals can hold up a new law for years while it is being appealed through the courts. All of this is also very expensive for the defendants and the taxpayer.

Federal judges should rule on if a law has been broken, or if a law is constitutional only. A judge at any level should not declare a new law as part of their rulings. Judges should also not be allowed to dictate what someone must do to be in compliance with his or her ruling.

Monuments

There has been a move lately to take down many of our statues and monuments. While it is true that some of these memorialized individuals that were less than perfect, they represent our history. You cannot erase the parts of history you dislike by trying to remove individuals in our history. Our nation *IS* our history! You learn from your nation's history so as not to repeat mistakes. To ignore it is to doom this nation to repeat it. If the believers in one political doctrine can remove monuments they do not like today, what is to stop the believers of another political doctrine from removing their monuments tomorrow?

What Happened?

Hillary Clinton has a legendary temper. When she lost the election, she lost her temper so badly she could not come out to address her supporters. Ever since then she has been trying to explain why she lost. She has come up with dozens of reasons, but refuses to face the fact that she is not very likable, people do not trust her, and she ran a terrible campaign.

Debt

They tell us on TV these days that if you do not pay your taxes or your credit card debt it is OK. Just call this number, and they will get you out of debt. Those of us that are responsible and pay our debts are the ones that pay the cost for these deadbeats in the long run.

The United Nations

Any discussion of US foreign relations must begin with the United Nations. The UN is the second attempt of world governments to form an organization to work out problems between countries. The League of Nations was formed after World War I, but it failed due in part to the United States not participating, but mostly because the "Great Powers" of the time were bent on promoting their own interests. The League fell apart with the onset of World War II.

After World War II many world leaders wanted to try it again with a new organization called the United Nations. Everyone was weary of war after two world wars in less than 50 years, and thought this might be a good idea as a way to solve problems before they lead to war. While the idea is laudable, it is like most liberal feel-good ideas. It was doomed to failure from the beginning. It has failed because it does not recognize human nature. It does not recognize that governments are led by politicians in one form or another. And politicians always look out for their own interests first. But even if you take the politicians out of the equation, it is only natural that each country would want what is in their best interest, and that will almost always be against the best interest of someone else. But because this is a liberal feel-good idea, and the liberals have influenced public opinion for so long, we have had the UN for over 50 years now.

The first problem with the UN was that it pitted what was then known as the free world against the communist world. What was called the third world then took whichever side they thought would benefit them. It became just a forum for finger pointing and name calling. Since the "security council" had both the US and the USSR as permanent members with veto power, it was guaranteed nothing significant would ever get done. However, without this veto power the organization would have fallen apart long ago. Countries like the US and USSR would never allow the UN to dictate policy to them.

Over the years the UN has created numerous agencies. Most are more than just worthless, they are jokes that waste money. Countries that are often the guiltiest of certain atrocities lead councils to stop the same atrocities. The UN "peacekeeping" forces have no real authority to enforce peace, and have in the past been guilty of crimes themselves. They supposedly fight world hunger by holding elaborate banquets to discuss the problem. They are all just little people enjoying living high on UN funds. And where do these funds come from? The US picks up a large portion of the entire operating costs of the UN. We finance an organization whose main purpose has become defying the US and working to its detriment. We even pay significant costs to protect and otherwise accommodate leaders of countries that come here to tell the UN and the world how bad we are.

While the UN has claimed authority to take grievances to world courts, neither the UN nor the world courts have any power to enforce anything. Any country can, and often does, ignore the UN when they do not like their findings or rules. In fact, I believe it is against the US Constitution for this country to cede any power or authority to another country or organization. The UN has sent peacekeeping forces into some countries that have no power to resist them, but they would never be able to do it in a country like China. They are even powerless to reign in countries like North Korea and Iran, even though they are member states.

In the past few decades, the UN has increasingly become an anti-Israeli, anti US, anti-western values organization. The smaller radical countries have banded together to have a party blaming us for all their problems. They not only expect us to take their rants and insults, they expect us to pay for the forum to do it. I am tired of pompous dictators like those idiots from Iran lecturing me on what is right. The UN outlived its usefulness long ago. We need to withdraw from the UN, stop any financial help, and give them no more than a year to relocate somewhere outside of the United States.

Antifa

The term "Antifa" is supposed to mean anti fascism. What is fascism?

fascism
noun fas·cism \ ˈfa-ˌshi-zəm *also* ˈfa-ˌsi- \

1 a political philosophy, movement, or regime (such as that of the Fascisti) that exalts nation and often race above the individual and that stands for a centralized **autocratic** government headed by a **dictatorial** leader, severe economic and social regimentation, and forcible suppression of opposition
2 a tendency toward or actual exercise of strong autocratic or dictatorial control
3 a way of organizing a society in which a government ruled by a dictator controls the lives of the people and in which people are not allowed to disagree with the government
4 very harsh control or authority
5 a political system headed by a dictator in which the government controls business and labor and opposition is not permitted

Sounds pretty bad. Who would not be antifascist? But are these people actually antifascist, or are they actually fascist themselves?

Look at number 1 above. They are expressing their belief there should be an autocratic government which will forcibly suppress any opposition to their beliefs.

Look at number 2. They want to take dictatorial control.

Look at number 3. They do not want to allow any disagreement with them.

Look at number 4. They want to harshly control any opposition.

Look at number 5. Opposition is not permitted.

They need to change their name to "Profa". They are acting very much like the black shirts of Mussolini.

Man vs. Woman

I suppose you could trace the feminist movement back as far as the women's suffrage movement, but I do not remember anything before the late 60's. It was about the time of Roe vs Wade that things seemed to break loose. That is when some women's groups started pushing the idea that women are equal to, if not superior to men.

Let me be perfectly clear about my position on the issue. I do not believe men are superior to women in general. Also, generally, women are not superior to men. But what the feminists refuse to admit is that a man and a woman are different, therefore not equal. Men can do some things better than women, and women can do some things better than men.

By insisting that women be treated as men's equals, they have succeeded in getting women into professions many are not suited for like police, firefighters, and the military. In order for them to qualify for these positions, standards had to be lowered. I have no problem with a woman police officer if she can protect me from a big burley man who wants to assault me. But do not send a small frail woman to do the job. If I am caught in a burning building, I want a firefighter capable of carrying me out if necessary.

Women can be surprisingly good at some jobs traditionally held by men. I used to work in heavy construction and know that women are usually better at operating heavy equipment than men. They can also be very good as electricians and welders. But most do not do well in jobs that require strength. It is just a fact that, in general, men are stronger than women.

Another thing. Other than a child born legitimately as a morphydite, everyone is born either male or female. I do not care if someone is not happy with what they are born, and has an operation; that cannot change it. They are still what they were born! Also, this nonsense of a male using a female restroom just because he says he "identifies" with being a female is just wrong.

There is more that I could say, but I will just leave it at what I have already said.

Beggars

I NEVER give money to someone begging on a street corner. These people make their living by begging rather than working. While it may be true that some cannot work and need help; to give them money assures that they will not get the real help they need. I think we need to bring back the vagrancy laws, and use them to force these people into shelters and other charities that can work to turn their lives around.

Keeping You Afraid

As I have previously said, the Socialist Democrats thrive on fear. That is the way they get votes. You need to be afraid of climate change, and only they can save you from it. You need to be afraid of the police, and only they can save you from it. If you are a woman you need to be afraid of losing your rights, and only they can save you from it. If you are a minority you need to be afraid of those racist Republicans, and only they can save you from it. You need to be afraid of Covid-19, and only they can save you from it. It is time that Americans stop living in fear and start enjoying this wonderful country.

The War on Poverty

In 1964, President Johnson declared war on poverty in the USA. His program was actually pretty successful for the first few years. But in spite of spending 22 trillion dollars (adjusted for inflation) over the past 50 years, the poverty level has flatlined for all these years. 22 trillion is 3 times the cost of all the military wars this country has ever fought.

One problem with "poverty" in this country is how your government defines poverty, and decides who gets government help. Consider the following facts about those the government has on the poverty roles.

- Eighty percent of poor households have air conditioning. By contrast, at the beginning of the War on Poverty, only about 12 percent of the entire U.S. population enjoyed air conditioning.
- Nearly three-quarters have a car or truck; 31 percent have two or more cars or trucks.
- Nearly two-thirds have cable or satellite television.
- Two-thirds have at least one DVD player, and a quarter have two or more.

- Half have a personal computer; one in seven has two or more computers.
- More than half of poor families with children have a video game system such as an Xbox or PlayStation.
- Forty-three percent have Internet access.
- Forty percent have a wide-screen plasma or LCD TV.
- A quarter have a digital video recorder system such as a TIVO.
- Ninety-two percent of poor households have a microwave.
- Ninety five percent are not homeless. Forty two percent own a home.
- Most report they are never hungry.

While I agree we need to be sure there is NO poverty on a country as rich as ours, we need to be sure we spend our money where it will do the most good. Usually, it can be argued that any government program is not a wise investment of money.

Full disclosure. I looked up much of the above online. I suppose some could argue the details, but it is still true that the governments "war on poverty" is a failure.

Winners and Losers

When I was young, I was not a very athletic boy. I was usually the last boy picked for a team and was the one they yelled "easy out" to when I came to bat. However, I am NOT in favor of the current thinking that there should not be any winners or losers in school sports. Sporting contests teach children that you cannot always win in everything you try. I learned to look elsewhere to find what I was good at and I am now more successful in life than some of the star athletes I knew in school.

Rock and Roll

Real rock and roll began around 1955. By 1975 it was gone. My teen years were in the early 1960s, so I was right in the middle of it. People born after that may enjoy listing to classic rock, but they can never really appreciate it like those of us who lived it.

<u>Money</u>

All money is earned by, belongs to, and is spent by individuals. No organization, either public or private has any money. Those in control of organizations do, however, spend money and determine how other individuals spend a great deal of money. Over time, people have become ignorant to basic economic facts because, I believe, economics is not taught in schools other than with a liberal slant.

The first organization to look at is government. Not just the federal government, but all levels. Any time you hear "the government" will pay for something, or something is a "free" government program translate that to mean you will pay for that with high taxes. Politicians have discovered they can buy your votes, using your money to pay for it, as long as you do not think of it as your money. They take your tax dollar, extract their cut in the form of salary and perks, spend the balance on some pork barrel program, and then convince you they did you a favor because they funneled "government money" into your district.

Still the politicians are not satisfied. They cannot buy enough votes with your tax dollar, so they borrow more money promising that you, not them, will repay it with interest. They tell you by approving bond sales they will not have to raise your taxes. The borrowed money is then spent on programs which make more people thankful to and dependent on the politicians.

The next type of organization to look at is the "non-profit" organization. While I appreciate organizations that help take care of those in need, too many of them are just political organizations that get away with not paying taxes. So, in a roundabout way, they too are using your tax dollar to influence political ends. Some are even given government "grants", (your money) to further their political agendas.

Let us look at business next. A business by itself does not earn or spend any money. It is merely a means by which individuals earn and spend money. Therefore, a business cannot and does not pay taxes. When the politicians raise taxes on businesses one of several thing happen. First the business can raise the price of their product to cover it, which is usually their first response. When this happens, you pay for it. If they cannot raise their prices enough, they lower the quality of their product. Again, in a roundabout way, you pay for it. If that is not enough, they lay off workers. This not only hurts the individuals who are laid off, but there are less taxes paid to fuel the politician's spending.

So, taxing of businesses is just another way of taxing the individual. The politicians know this, but they want you to believe that by taxing the businesses they are helping to relieve your tax burden.

The last group to look at are the hard-core welfare recipients. They are the people that have learned to work the system. They have never contributed to society, and never intend to do so. But these people vote. So, here again, the politicians have an interest in keeping your tax dollar supporting these individuals.

While there are legitimate things the government does that needs your money to pay for, it is high time to reign in the politician's spending. Politicians are elected to serve the people, not to rule over them and certainly not to rob them.

How I Vote

I have only voted for a president two times in my life. Ronald Reagan – second term, and Donald Trump – second term. Don't get me wrong. I go to the polls every national election. But both the parties put up such bad candidates, I find myself in the position of voting against what I consider to be the worst of the two. You ask why don't I vote for a third-party candidate? That is just throwing your vote away and possibly helping the worst one win. Ross Perot got Bill Clinton elected – twice.

<u>**Texas Teachers**</u>

Many years back, Texas passed a law that said public school teachers must pass a test showing they had enough knowledge of the subject they taught, to teach it. Sounds reasonable. But Texas was immediately sued because it was said the law discriminated against black teachers. About that time, I was called to jury duty and while waiting to see if I would be picked, I started talking to a school teacher. I told her I did not understand what the suit was about and she explained it this way. There are several large black universities in Texas. It seems they were virtually giving away degrees to students that did not earn them. The reasoning was that blacks were underrepresented in jobs that required a degree. Most of them still could not get a job anywhere because of their lack of the knowledge required to perform, but schools would hire them to teach. This teacher told me that many of them could not even read and write well.

I do not remember how the lawsuit turned out, but I will say that ALL colleges and universities these days seem to be giving away degrees to students that do not earn them. I know this to be true because I have one hanging on the wall in front of me as I write this. But I am not claiming the ability to teach.

Socialism in America

An entire book could be written on this subject, so forgive me if I do not cover everything in detail.

While some forms of socialistic thought go way back, I am going to start with the period between WWI and WWII. During that time, it became popular for the rich and the elite to embrace communism. The theories of Karl Marx sounded good to them, but had not been tested. However, all Marx really espoused was a socialist dictatorship. Once most of the people of the world rejected communism, the elite turned to just socialism. At least that is what they said openly. They knew that the only way true socialism would work is for the government to take total control. A dictatorship.

FDR was one of these socialists. He took advantage of the great depression to push his socialist beliefs. He admired the socialist Benito Mussolini in Italy, and even Adolf Hitler at first. He convinced the American people he could lift them out of the depression, and blamed the depression on the failures of his predecessor and capitalism. The press were his willing accomplices, being elite socialists themselves. It is my belief that the era of FDR ushered in the socialist movement in earnest. (*I have written a separate book on this.*)

The problem they had was that socialism was a hard sell to the average person back then. Enter Cloward-Piven. Richard Cloward and Francis Piven were two sociology professors at Columbia University who, back in 1966 advanced a strategy to force socialism on the US. Their idea was that you could hasten the fall of capitalism by overloading the US government with welfare and other expensive social programs thereby forcing us into a financial collapse. Their theory was that at that point the American people would welcome socialism as the only answer to save the country. They specifically said that the Republicans would never accept their plan, and looked to the Democrats to bring it to reality. Since that time, the Democrats (with the help of some Republicans) have slowly turned the US into welfare state. They thought they had finally succeeded with the election of President Obama. Obama followed their strategy to the tee.

Look at what Forbes reported happened in 2012 under the Obama watch.

- An increase of 18 million people, to 46 million Americans receiving food stamps;
- A 122 percent increase in food-stamp spending to an estimated $89 billion this year from $40 billion in 2008;
- An increase of 3.6 million people receiving Social Security disability payments;
- A 10 million person increase in the number of individuals receiving welfare, to 107 million, or more than one-third of the U.S. population;
- A 34 percent, $683 billion reduction in the adjusted gross income of the top 1 percent to $1.3 trillion in 2009 (latest data) from its 2007 peak
- Federal expenditures on Obamacare will total $2.3 trillion, a $1.4 trillion increase from the program's initial estimates;
- The combination of budget cuts and sequestration will reduce defense spending by $1 trillion, while total government spending will increase by $1.1 trillion;
- Taxes will be increased by $1.8 trillion;
- Yet, the national debt will increase by another $11 trillion

I know the Democrats will deny they had any plans to knowingly bankrupt our country, but the only other explanation for their behavior would be total stupidity. If the above could not be helped, then how could President Trump turn it around so quickly? Remember when Obama said the lack of manufacturing jobs was "the new normal" and we would just have to accept it?

The Democrats under Biden are now reversing every good thing President Trump did. They appear to be trying to quickly bankrupt America before the American people take them out of power.

Everyone reading this needs to research Cloward-Piven on the internet. Do not take my word for it. It will open many eyes.

Eddie Aiken

I grew up in El Paso, Texas, and went to school in the Ysleta school district. The schools have never been segregated in that district but there was an all-black high school in the El Paso district before WWII. It was not because of a lack of racial prejudice, but simply because there were not enough black children to justify having separate schools. When I was a freshman in high school, there was a black boy that was a senior. When I was a senior, there was a black girl that was a freshman. I was aware that my parents were prejudiced, but it was something that rarely came up. I remember when the blacks entered the all-white colleges in the south, and I could not figure out what all the fuss was about. Most of the blacks in El Paso were in the military, or stayed here when they retired because they liked that there was so little prejudice here.

When I started my first job at the age of 17, there was a black man that was the janitor. His name was Eddie Aiken. Eddie was a short, stocky man with the largest hands I have ever seen. He was a boxer while in the military, and I swear his fists looked like anvils. But he never showed any signs of being combative or aggressive. In fact, he was always smiling and a very pleasant person. Eddie was my very first experience with a black person, and it was a very positive one.

I moved to Houston, Texas when I was 21. Houston had a lot of black people, but that did not bother me. I got along well with everyone I worked with and became friends with many black men and women. But, over time I came to realize that there was something about their culture that kept them at arm's length from me. It was not me; it was them. As time went by, I began to have fewer and fewer black friends. I have to admit, I was also influenced some by all the prejudiced people in the area. But I always wanted to treat people fairly, no matter their heritage.

Then I took a short job in St. Croix, USVI. That place, like most of the Caribbean is about 80% black. Most of the blacks there hate white people, and do not try to hide it. I learned firsthand what it was like to experience real prejudice and to want to return the feeling.

Today, when I think of racial prejudice, my first reaction is to go back to St. Croix. But then when I think about it, I go back to Eddie Aiken.

<u>FDR Was The Beginning</u>

I have said in a previous chapter that FDR was the beginning of the modern socialist movement. But there was another, just as sinister thing that began with FDR.

The stock market crashed in 1929 under the administration of Herbert Hoover. This, along with other factors brought on the great depression in 1930. Hoover was not that good of a President, and could have done some things better regarding the economy. However, he DID NOT do anything to cause the depression.

When FDR ran for president, he blamed Hoover and the Republicans for all the nations woes. He promised that he could solve the problem. After he was elected, he continued to blame Hoover. He referred to the homeless camps as "Hoovervilles", and renamed a dam being built on the Colorado river from Hoover Dam to Boulder Dam. (Fortunately, people with better sense renamed it back to Hoover Dam later.) Although FDR had some initial success in turning things around, it did not last because government control of the economy never works for long. However, FDR became wildly popular, and seen as our nation's savior. The more the people worshipped at the throne of Saint FDR, the easier it was to demonize all Republicans. This has carried on to this day, getting worse with each Republican administration.

The first Republican president after FDR was Dwight D. Eisenhower. Eisenhower was very popular as the leader of the allied forces in Europe that defeater Hitler. The Democrats tried to recruit he to run for the presidency as a Democrat. But, when he ran and won as a Republican, they reverted to their FDR ways. The Democrats, and the news media who were by this time totally devoted to the democrats because of their reverence to saint FDR, turned on the war hero, Eisenhower, and unfairly painted him as a terrible president.

The next Republican president was Richard Nixon. Nixon had two problems. First, he was a Republican, and next he was a crooked politician. Being crooked was not bad in the eyes of the media and Democrats. If that was so, the previous two Democrat presidents were worse that Nixon. But being a Republican and getting caught at being crooked was enough to bring him down.

Ronald Reagan came next. Because of their success at bringing down Nixon, the Democrats and their willing accomplices in the media came down hard on Reagan. However, Reagan was the most popular president since saint FDR. The press backed off some when he was almost assassinated, but mostly throughout his presidency, he was ridiculed as a buffoon.

Next came Bush one. By this point the Democrats and the leftist media were becoming experts at demonizing anyone who opposed them. The same was true of Bush two.

President Donald J. Trump has more than the problem of just being a Republican. He beat Hillary, who the left was putting all their hopes in to continue, and hopefully finish, what Obama started. That was unforgivable. He was also not a politician. He was not part of the DC elite. He also planned to actually do something about getting this country back on track, not just talk about it. But the very worst thing was, he did not talk like a politician. He called out both Democrats and Republicans for their stupidity. The Democrats and the media went into full battle mode to bring Trump down.

Look now at how history has been written. The Democrats and the media HATE a sitting Republican president. They IGNORE a living Republican ex-president. And they LOVE a dead Republican ex-president.

It all started with FDR.

Since finishing this book, I have written another book titled "FDR – Satan or Saint". It lays out exactly how FDR changed the political landscape in our country for the worse.

<u>Iran</u>

I am certainly no expert on either Iranian history or everything pertaining Iran today. However, I do know enough to have some opinions.

When I was growing up Iran was ruled by the Shah of Iran. Shah basically means king. He had some very high aspirations of what he wanted his country to be. He initiated numerous reforms to westernize his country. He built many schools and universities which he made available to all. This raised the literacy rate dramatically in the country. There was high economic growth in Iran because of his policies. Women were not only allowed to be educated, but they were given the right to drive a car and even vote. Iran under the Shah became very prosperous, and Iran was also very pro-western.

In spite of all these "improvements", there was significant resistance to his rule both in Iran and with those who were supposed to be his allies like the U.S. and Great Briton. While John and Robert Kennedy, and later Jimmy Carter made no secret they did not like him, the CIA helped the Shah with dealing with his opponents.

If he was doing so much good for his country, why did he have such opposition? The Muslim clerics did not like the westernization of their country, and especially disapproved of giving rights to women. The Shah arrested and imprisoned his critics, and there have been credible accusations of torture. Many of the clerics fled the country, but they smuggled their sermons into the country on tapes. One of his chief critics was the Ayatollah Khomeini.

The Shah developed cancer, and in early 1979 he left the country for medical treatment. He knew at the time he would not return. As soon as he left, a revolution occurred and his rule was overthrown and the Ayatollah Khomeini was put in charge. Jimmy Carter did nothing to interfere. He, like so many these days think that to replace any dictator with someone the people want is good. But this time it turned into a disaster. Then, when the Shah came to the U.S. for medical treatment the new government in Iran demanded the U.S. send him back to Iran for trial. Carter refused, which made the Iranians more anti U.S. A group of students in Iran stormed the U.S. embassy and took everyone hostage. The Ayatollah was terrified according to a later interview with his son. He just knew the U.S. would attack Iran and he would be removed. But days went by and Carter did nothing. Then weeks. Then months. Finally, the Ayatollah realized nothing would happen and openly backed the students.

When the Ayatollah, which was then the government of Iran, backed the students he broke international law. Any embassy in any country is considered sovereign soil of that country. To attack our embassy is to attack our country. It was an act of war. Still Carter did nothing.

Carter finally tried to send in a mission to rescue the hostages, but that ended in disaster when an accident brought down a helicopter that collided with a support plane. The Iranians paraded the burned, dead bodies of American soldiers in the streets of Tehran. The Ayatollah told his people that this was proof that Allah was on their side and the U.S. was just a paper tiger.

Presidents Reagan, Bush 1, Clinton, and Bush 2 did nothing as matters got worse and Iran became the number 1 state sponsor of terrorism in the world. Then President Obama seemed to actively work to help the Iranians by making a deal with them that included giving them billions of dollars. Think of this. Iran is the number 1 state sponsor of terrorism, calls the U.S. the "great Satan" and has openly called for the destruction of Israel, and Obama gave them billions of dollars to help pay for all their deeds.

I do not know what the answer is, but this should have been resolved long ago.

The Difference

The difference between a Republican and a Democrat is this. A Republican sees a person in a ditch and reaches out his hand to help him out of the ditch. A Democrat sees a person in a ditch and throws him a few crumbs to help him survive in the ditch, and expects him to be grateful.

My Way

As I have thought about what subjects to write in my book, I kept coming back to the idea of "what it is to be an American". Unfortunately, the more I thought about it, the more I realized there is no good description of an American, and many of the citizens of my country are not, in my opinion, good examples of what an American should be. I have decided to finish my book with this on what it would be like to be an American, if I had my way. You feminist will have to forgive my use of "he" and "his" to describe an American. I do it only to make it easier.

This is what an American would be if I had my way.

An American is proud of his country. He believes in American exceptionalism. But he is not arrogant about it. He wants to help others in the world, but understands there are those who will never achieve what we have and do not appreciate our help. An American is not foolish enough to think we can buy friends.

An American is a person who believes in the rule of law. An American puts the Constitution of the United States first, then obeys all laws that had been passed for the good of the country and society. If an American disagrees with a law, he works to peaceably convince others of the need to change the law. An American never uses his disagreement with a law or court verdict as an excuse to riot, destroy property, or murder. An American believes in the justice system and takes his responsibility to serve on juries or testify in court hearings seriously, and does not try to get out of these duties.

An American is a person who believes in education. He understands that an educated person makes a better citizen and he continues through life to do everything within his power to continue to learn and better himself. He knows and understands the Constitution of the United States and how our government is supposed to work. He will not tolerate anyone trying to distort facts to keep people ignorant of the truth. He supports public education, but demands excellence in teachers and does not tolerate abuse in the educational system to indoctrinate children and young people in political beliefs.

An American understands what a right is, and demands that his rights and the rights of others are protected. He will not tolerate any attempt to deny anyone their constitutional rights. He does not believe in political correctness as he realizes this is an attempt to restrict free speech. He tries to be considerate of others in his own speech within reason. He is not tolerant of those who use free speech to distort the truth.

An American believes that whatever religious beliefs another has is their own business as long as it does not promote anything harmful to others. An American has the right to try to convince others to change to their point of view as long as he does not try to force anything on anyone. An American understands the first amendment is there to protect his right to the free exercise of his beliefs or religion, not to limit his rights or those of others.

An American understands what capitalism is, and accepts that he lives in a capitalist system. He works within the system to succeed to the best of his abilities, but understands that this system allows some to prosper more than others. He does not take advantage of the system to cheat others, and will not tolerate others doing so. He understands that any intervention in the natural order of capitalism, whether from the government or others is counterproductive and harmful in the long run.

An American is part of the American culture. While he may be proud of his foreign heritage, he puts being an American first. An American does not care what the color of another's skin is, or the country of his or his ancestor's origin, or his religion, as long as the person is a fellow American. An American realizes our society may include some customs and beliefs of other cultures, but a true American sees that as only a meld that makes the American culture that we are all part of. Part of the American culture is we all share a common language – English. There is no such thing as a minority culture in America. We are all Americans. An American understands that to recognize certain groups as minorities deserving separate treatment or privileges destroys our culture as one people.

An American understands there will always be those who will not fit into society. He supports the right of society to protect itself with laws and punishment, and the right of the individual to reasonably protect himself, his family, and his property. He understands the police cannot be everywhere, so citizens have a right to use firearms to protect themselves when necessary. He understands that with this right comes responsibilities and a citizen may be punished by law for any irresponsible use of a firearm.

An American respects the right of every person in the United States to life, and to live it peaceably. The only exception is when a person is judged by a court of law to be removed from society by jail or execution. An American protects the life of the innocent and those who cannot protect themselves, including those who have not yet been born.

An American understands the importance of protecting our country from those who would do us harm, or steal from us, or take advantage of us. An American supports our law enforcement at all levels, our military, and our border protection officers. But he will not tolerate corruption in any of these agencies. An American understands that while it is sad that there is so much poverty in other parts of the world, we cannot allow them all to come here as we cannot afford to support them as it will only bring down the living standards for all current citizens.

An American knows that he must do his part to support his government through taxes. However, he demands that government at all levels be responsible in how these taxes are collected and spent. He does not tolerate politicians who believe they can use tax monies for political advantage. He does not tolerate government waste of the people's money.

Most importantly, an American Votes! But he is an educated voter. He studies the issues to understand them and determine which are most important. He learns all there is to know about the candidates to determine who is the most qualified. He puts what is best for the country first ahead of party affiliation or other considerations. He is not influenced by things that do not matter like race, religion, or how well the person looks and talks on TV. He understands that a politician will often lie, and the press will often misrepresent the truth, so he is diligent to find out the facts. An American respects the outcome of an election unless there is evidence of fraud. An American will not tolerate voter fraud. And finally, an American understands that when a mistake is made any politician may be removed from office on the next election or by other processes like impeachment.

If I had my way…

<u>Danny Westbrook</u>

When my wife and I married, she had a son named Danny Westbrook. As he grew up his father introduced him to alcohol, drugs, and prostitutes. Danny's life spiraled downward until he died at the age of 51. His mother wrote this poem.

My Favorite Son

My favorite son you will always be
From birth through eternity
Tho broken in this life no fault could I ever see
As our Lord Jesus gave Himself for you and me

Bonded from birth with God's eternal love
I know we will be reunited in our heavenly home above
Your true heart of gold was revealed to many who told
Of giving of yourself as you walked along that lonely road

Eyes that saw others who suffered pain and grief
Your heart was open to help bring them relief

Though troubled and broken you always had
faith
That one day you would surely walk through
God's pearly gate

An earthly home you always sought
But that heavenly home you knew had been
bought
With the blood of Jesus on that cruel cross
You knew for sure God would not count you as
lost

So, rest in peace my favorite son.

Amen

About the Author

Robert Allan Dobbin was born in El Paso, Texas in 1946. He graduated high school in 1964, and began attending Texas Western College, (now the University of Texas at El Paso.) He did not graduate, but left college for a short stay in Fort Worth, Texas, then moved to Houston, Texas in 1968.

Robert married Sandria Sue Boshell Westbrook in 1973. The job he had gave them the opportunity to travel all over the U.S. They have lived and worked from Florida to Washing State – Delaware to California – Hawaii to the US Virgin Islands, and many places in between. He and his wife eventually returned to El Paso to retire. They have a daughter living in Arizona.

Robert and Sandria continue to travel some, and otherwise enjoy life. They are both artists in oil painting, and Robert enjoys photography. The cover photo was taken by Robert.

www.ingramcontent.com/pod-product-compliance
Lightning Source LLC
Chambersburg PA
CBHW061748250726

48657CB00001B/50